Naval Historical Foundation

Manuscript Collection

A Catalog

LIBRARY OF CONGRESS   WASHINGTON   1974

Naval Historical Foundation
Building 220, Room 218
Washington Navy Yard
Washington, D.C. 20390

The Naval Historical Foundation wishes to thank Mrs. Renée Charlotte Debié Oberlin, deceased widow of Captain Edgar Garfield Oberlin, U.S.N., for the generous bequest which made this catalog possible.

Library of Congress Cataloging in Publication Data

United States. Library of Congress.
Naval Historical Foundation manuscript collection.

Supt. of Docs. no.: LC 1.2: N22/2
1. United States—History, Naval—Sources—
Bibliography—Catalogs. 2. United States.
Library of Congress. 3. Naval Historical
Foundation. I. Naval Historical Foundation.
II. Title.
Z1249.N3U5 1974   016.359'00973   74-1373
ISBN 0-8444-0119-6

For sale by the Superintendent of Documents, U.S. Government Printing Office
Washington, D.C. 20402 – Price $5.05
Stock Number 3003-00015

W. S. DeLany
Vice Admiral, U.S. Navy (Ret.)
President
Naval Historical Foundation

THE NAVAL HISTORICAL FOUNDATION is a nonprofit organization which was chartered in the District of Columbia in 1926. Its main objectives are to collect and preserve private documents, papers, and artifacts of naval historical significance and to make them readily available for public display and scholarly research; to stimulate the study of naval history, naval customs, and naval traditions; and to portray the role of seapower in the development of the United States. Since its beginning the foundation has been endorsed by the Secretary of the Navy and the Chief of Naval Operations. The SECNAV and CNO have supported the foundation's goals, emphasized its objectives as being in the best interest of the Navy, and approved the foundation as the proper repository for private papers relating to the Navy.

The foundation received its first acquisitions in 1926. Among them were issues of the Boston *Repertory*, dated 12 and 15 May 1804, and 13 manuscript documents of May 1813 relating to gunboat administration. By 1949 its acquisitions had grown to such an extent that their sheer volume exceeded the facilities available to the foundation for their use. An agreement was therefore concluded with the Library of Congress that significant collections would be placed on deposit in the Manuscript Division of the Library. The collections remained there in their "raw," unprocessed condition until 1965. The foundation then entered into an agreement with the Library to have the collections cataloged and indexed to facilitate their usefulness to the growing number of interested researchers. At that time there were approximately 200,000 items in the collections, and it was estimated that the project would take about three years to complete. Because the foundation retained ownership of the collections, it paid for the processing work done by the Library's staff. To defray this expense, a committee of 39 interested civilians sponsored a fund drive which raised about 75 percent of the needed capital.

The Naval Historical Foundation collection now contains about 337,000 items, which have been indexed and cataloged in 254 separate collections. Thirty-six of the most significant collections have been described in great detail in published registers. More collections will be added as the foundation continues its work of collecting naval papers. The foundation hopes that the publication of this catalog will be a major step in the growth of this project and that, as scholars continue to use these collections as source material in naval history, the value and significance of the collection will increase.

HANSON W. BALDWIN
Consulting and Roving Editor, *Reader's Digest*
Formerly Military Editor, *New York Times*

THE NAVAL HISTORICAL FOUNDATION, headed by a distinguished group of blue-water seamen who understand that a man's, or a Navy's, past is not only prologue but also the firm foundation for the present and future, has accumulated the largest single collection of personal naval papers in the nation. Now deposited in the Library of Congress and indexed and cross-referenced for research, this collection of papers, documents, and memorabilia has been sorted and cataloged with such technical skill and devoted detail that it forms the Comstock Lode of U.S. naval history. Its fame should spread far beyond the circle of students who have so far consulted it. In fact, all serious researchers in nearly every aspect of naval history must, in the future, consult these files before they can consider their work complete.

The collection goes back to our nation's beginnings and covers all the seas and most of the nations of yesterday and today. Each researcher will be able to indulge a catholicity of taste. To this writer, however, the more recent acquisitions—though as yet ungilded by the patina of time—are the most interesting and important. For in each man's life, it has been sadly but truly said, there is one war, one great conflict, which touched him far more intimately, moved him far more emotionally, involved him far more intellectually, than any other conflict of his time. For me this war was World War II. Future historians of this conflict and future biographers of its leaders will find a rich mine of fact and opinion relating to its background in the extensive papers of Admirals Ernest J. King, William F. Halsey, Claude C. Bloch, John F. Shafroth, and Frederick J. Horne, and these collections will soon be enhanced by the addition of Admiral Nimitz' papers.

In the Horne papers, for example, readers will discover Admiral Horne's down-to-earth, "old shoe" personality, his tremendous loyalty to the Navy and the nation, and his clear understanding of public relations in the best sense. Admiral Horne was a man who compensated for and complemented, to the great benefit of the country, the characteristics, capabilities, and personality of Admiral King. Through several years of the war I was privileged to be one of a very small group of trusted newspapermen who were told by Admiral Horne not only what the Navy had done but what it hoped for and what it intended to do. The result, I was convinced then and am even more convinced now, was invaluable to the Navy. Admiral Horne's papers, although they represent only a small part of the foundation's collections, are certain to provide new dimensions in any study of the war years.

This rich lode of documents, supplemented in time by future donations, will clothe with flesh and blood the official papers and the oral history accounts in the Navy's Operational Archives. The result should enable future historians to tell the Navy's story and to tell it "like it was," with the facts of war almost as naked as they were in the clash of battle.

EDWIN B. HOOPER
Vice Admiral, U.S. Navy (Ret.)
Director of Naval History

As DIRECTOR OF NAVAL HISTORY I often recall the observation of Alfred Thayer Mahan that naval historians "limit themselves generally to the duty of simple chroniclers of naval occurrences." There are exceptions, but the tendency is still evident, perhaps encouraged in part by the discrete nature of ships, the glamour of their adventures on the ever-changing seas, and the individuality each seems to develop. Yet the story is incomplete unless it weaves in the officers and men who give life to their ships and whose decisions and actions determine the outcome of operations on, under, and over seas. Similarly important are the individuals in headquarters and supporting activities.

In this respect official records, such as those in the National Archives, the Navy's Operational Archives, and the Federal Records Centers, tell but part of the story. Moreover, official reports have tended over the years to become more stylized and formal, more stilted, more cryptic, and more restrained. The human element tends to be neglected, both in relation to operations and to the decision process. In regard to planning and operations, the main emphasis quite naturally is on war and combat actions—often without balanced treatment of comparably important activities of the Navy and its personnel under conditions other than war.

In short, the significance of personal papers of naval men goes well beyond that of their obvious biographical value. Unless researchers draw upon such papers as a complement to those of an official nature, the true history of the Navy and of naval events and their significance will not be revealed.

The richest source of personal papers related to the U.S. Navy is the extensive collection of the Naval Historical Foundation, deposited in the Library of Congress. This catalog, with its summary information on the papers and its cross-indexing with regard to personalities and subjects, serves as a complement to the registers on individual groups of papers and greatly enhances the utility of the foundation's valuable collections.

There are serious gaps in the recording and interpreting of U.S. naval history. It is hoped that this catalog, with Dr. Heffron's excellent introduction highlighting a number of research opportunities and the perceptive essays of Vice Admiral DeLany, Professor Merrill, and Mr. Baldwin, will stimulate the filling of many of these gaps.

James M. Merrill
Professor of History and Marine Studies
University of Delaware

NAVAL HISTORY AS A RECOGNIZED AREA of U.S. history is of relatively recent origin, but it is also one of the fastest growing fields for research and writing. Shortly after World War II a generation of naval historians began publishing a fresh flow of monographic studies based on solid and exhaustive research in the manuscript sources. Articles on naval subjects began appearing with greater frequency in learned journals. Theses and dissertations increased yearly. Library shelves now have respectable sections for books relating to naval studies. Colleges and universities are implanting naval and maritime history in their curricula. Several universities have established colleges of marine studies.

The scholar's patient and constant quest for manuscript material is by no means concentrated on the official records housed in the National Archives. Researchers have a deep interest in personal papers of individuals who held top commands and, to a lesser degree, in the correspondence of their subordinates.

As the Naval Historical Foundation's collection is the best single source of personal papers, historians are grateful to have a comprehensive, printed catalog of the holdings, instead of having to plow through the overly used, although useful, typewritten copy of the contents of the collection, which was available only at the Manuscript Division, Library of Congress. As an indispensable tool, this well-indexed catalog will spur research. The collection contains a valuable reservoir of materials for literally hundreds of theses, dissertations, and books.

Among the more significant groups of papers in the Naval Historical Foundation's collection are the papers of Stephen Luce, Thomas Selfridge, David Dixon Porter, and Robert W. Shufeldt. Perhaps the most important group of letters for the 19th century are those of John Rodgers, whose illustrious career spanned 52 years. Boxes contain his private and official correspondence, logbooks, notebooks, memoranda, newspaper clippings, drafts of manuscripts, and assorted miscellaneous material. Although Rodgers did not keep copies of his outgoing letters, some of his original letters, most of them addressed to members of his family, are preserved here. His papers document his activities as a high-ranking naval officer whose assignments included duty in nearly all types of ships. His collection is particularly noteworthy in that it records his impressions of the transition from a wooden to an iron-ship navy. Topics about which he wrote were many and varied and illuminate the Navy's role during the 19th century. During his years in the service, the absence of censorship permitted him to write his wife with frankness and candor, and he wrote her almost every day.

Other significant papers in the Naval Historical Foundation collection are those of Washington Irving Chambers, a pioneer in naval aviation. This collection can be roughly divided into two parts: first, the pre-1910 material, which is generally concerned with Chambers' career and activities as an officer both ashore and afloat; second, the post-1910 correspondence, which deals primarily with Chambers' interest in the fast-growing field of naval aviation and his importance as one of its leaders.

Among the finest collections for the World War II period are the papers of Admiral William F. Halsey. They contain war diaries, narratives of campaigns, operational plans, orders, and newspaper clippings, but perhaps most significant for the scholar are the packets of personal letters and the correspondence with Admiral Chester Nimitz, which reveal the inner thoughts of Halsey.

The serious researcher is indeed indebted to the Naval Historical Foundation and the Library of Congress for jointly publishing this catalog, an outstanding contribution to the field of naval history.

PAUL T. HEFFRON
Manuscript Historian
Library of Congress

CONSISTING OF OVER 250 INDIVIDUAL COLLECTIONS and extending in time from the close of the American Revolution through the period of World War II, the Naval Historical Foundation collection is the largest body of personal papers in a single repository relating to American naval history. These papers provide historians with original source material for a wide variety of studies. Here is the unfolding story of strategy and tactics in wars declared and undeclared, of the development of naval architecture, ordnance, engineering, communications, submarines, and aviation. All of these subjects, of course, take on larger dimensions and fuller meaning when viewed through the lives of the individual naval officers behind them. Their biographies in many instances remain to be written, and for this purpose the collection is a primary and rewarding archive.

Beyond its usefulness for conventional naval history and biography, the collection is a valuable supplementary source for those working in the field of American diplomacy. Naval officers often doubled as diplomatic agents, reporting back to Washington on political conditions from their stations in Latin America, Africa, China—indeed, from wherever the fleet may have been operating. Social historians as well will find useful material in the collection. Diaries and family letters, for example, record impressions of foreign lands and peoples, revealing at the same time the habits of American seamen and the customs and discipline of the service. For the student of domestic political history and public administration, many of the papers will suggest the influence of naval officers and private interest groups upon Congress and the naval committees in formulating the nation's naval policies and programs. Historians of science, in turn, will be attracted to such segments of the collection as the records of the Naval Observatory.

A few collections may be singled out because of their special potential for research on subjects needing further and more definitive treatment. Two of these relate to the interesting fields of naval aviation and communications. In the papers of Washington Irving Chambers the researcher will encounter the most important single group of documents on the evolution of naval aviation. A complementary collection on this same subject, which should not be overlooked, is that of John Lansing Callan, another pioneer in aviation. Stanford C. Hooper, not inaccurately described as the father of navy radio, fortunately preserved a substantial body of papers which are indispensable for tracing the development of the Navy's highly successful system of communications.

Naval administrative reorganization was a subject of intense debate from the opening of the Naval War College in 1884 to the establishment of the Office of Chief of Naval Operations in 1915. In the forefront of the fight to reorganize the Navy Department were Stephen B. Luce, William F. Fullam, and William S. Sims. Their papers introduce the reader to the enormous internal pressures confronting the so-called insurgents in their efforts to make the Navy a more effective fighting force. The Sims papers, together with those of Albert Gleaves, also afford a more complete picture of the Navy's role in World War I. For significant aspects of global strategy in World War II and the great Pacific fleet battles, the papers of Ernest J. King and William F. Halsey are obviously basic.

A brief introduction cannot do justice to the total research value of the Naval Historical Foundation collection. The comprehensiveness of the collection, however, may be seen in the descriptive card catalog, and its content is explained with greater particularity in the registers to individual papers. Moreover, its full potential will be realized when studied in conjunction with the many related collections acquired by the Library of Congress from individual donors. Among the most prominent of these are the papers of such naval officers as John Paul Jones, John Barry, Matthew Fontaine Maury, Alfred Thayer Mahan, George Dewey, and William D. Leahy. Researchers should also be directed to the papers of 23 Presidents and many Secretaries of the Navy in the Manuscript Division. Finally, all of this rare material is complemented by the Library's unparalleled collection of books, journals, pamphlets, newspapers, prints, and photographs. The bringing together of these sources in a single repository offers scholars unique opportunities and challenges.

Contents

Manuscript Collection

Babbitt, Edward B.,   d. 1840
Journals, 1828–31. 2 v.
Naval officer. Official journals kept by Babbitt on board the U.S.F. Guerrière and U.S.S. Dolphin, Pacific Squadron.
Deposited by the Naval Historical Foundation, 1958.

Bainbridge, William,   1774–1833
Correspondence, 1804–28. 8 items.
Naval officer. Letters of Bainbridge to Henry A. S. Dearborn, Thomas Harris, and John Ridgely, chiefly concerning incidents in his career with annotations added by Arthur Bainbridge Hoff (1869–1935). Also a letter to Bainbridge from his niece, Mary B. Maclean.
Deposited by the Naval Historical Foundation, 1964.

Baldridge, Harry Alexander,   1880–1952
Papers, 1902–47. 100 items.
Naval officer. Correspondence, including letters from William H. Standley concerning Haiti (1930); Baldridge's reports from Haiti (1930); orders to duty; and two articles by Baldridge. Other correspondents are John R. Beardsall and Husband E. Kimmel.
Deposited by the Naval Historical Foundation, 1964.

Barron, James,   1769–1851
Correspondence, 1831–49. 57 items.
Naval officer. Correspondence, chiefly circulars received from the U.S. Board of Navy Commissioners and signed by John Rodgers and William A. Harris, relating to Barron's duties as commanding officer of the U.S Navy Yard, Philadelphia. Subjects include ship construction, outfitting and repairs, appropriations, and the defense of the yard. Other correspondents include Samuel M. Barclay and Samuel Burch.
Deposited by the Naval Historical Foundation, 1955, 1957.

Bates, John A.,   d. 1871
Papers, 1849–53. 1 v. (ca. 110 p.)
Purser in the U.S. Navy. Watch, quarter, and station bill for the brig

Perry, with enclosures consisting of a letter to Bates concerning bounty, naval orders, and newspaper clippings.
Deposited by the Naval Historical Foundation, 1964.

Bates, Richard Waller, 1892–
Collection, 1780–1865. 18 items.
Naval officer and autograph collector. Consists of signed autograph letters of William Bainbridge, Henry E. Ballard, Isaac Chauncey, James Fenimore Cooper, John H. Dent, David Porter, John Rodgers, and others, chiefly concerning naval matters.
Deposited by the Naval Historical Foundation, 1961.

Beardslee, Lester Anthony, 1836–1903
Papers, 1850–1900. 128 items.
Naval officer. Journal kept on board the U.S.S. Wachusett in 1864 during blockade duty in the Civil War; letter (1885) from James E. Jouett relating to the restoration of order in Panama; orders to duty; and an invitation. Journal entries concern discipline on board ship, ports of call, and the boarding of foreign ships.
Deposited by the Naval Historical Foundation, 1967.

Belknap, George Eugene, 1832–1903
Papers, 1857–1903. 1400 items.
Naval officer and author. Correspondence, articles, memoranda, and miscellaneous papers, relating to Belknap's naval career which included duty in Canton, China, the Civil War, Hawaii, and command of the Asiatic Fleet, and to his interest in hydrography, oceanography, family genealogy, old sea stories, and social, economic, and political questions. Correspondents include members of his family, Daniel Ammen, John Mercer Brooke, Caspar F. Goodrich, Samuel W. Lowell, Francis Asbury Roe, George Collier Remey, and John A. Riddle.
Register published by the Library in 1969.
Deposited by the Naval Historical Foundation, 1959.

Belknap, Reginald Rowan, 1871–1959
Papers, 1784–1929. 7100 items.
Naval officer and author. Correspondence, financial and legal records, photos, newspaper clippings, and printed matter. Primarily correspondence (1900–29) on personal and social matters between Belknap and his family.
Register published by the Library in 1969.
Deposited by the Naval Historical Foundation, 1959.

Bell, Henry Haywood, 1808–1868
Order, 1866. 1 item.

Naval officer. General order reporting the court-martial of James Smith, which was convened by Bell, commander, East India squadron.
Deposited by the Naval Historical Foundation, 1964.

Bellamy, John Haley,　1836–1914
Collection, 1941. 7 items.
Wood carver. Biographical sketch and two photos of Bellamy, creator of the U.S.S. Lancaster's eagle figurehead.
Deposited by the Naval Historical Foundation, 1964.

Bennett, Frank Marion,　1857–1924
Papers, 1893–1909. 200 items.
Naval officer and author. Chiefly testimonial letters and newspaper and magazine reviews of Bennett's books The Steam Navy of the United States (1896) and The Monitor and the Navy Under Steam (1900).
Finding aid in the Library.
Deposited by the Naval Historical Foundation, 1964.

Billings, Luther Guiteau,　1842–1922
Collection, 1865–1900. 12 items.
Naval officer. Two articles by Billings concerning, in part, his experiences during the Civil War in the U.S. Navy and as a prisoner of war in Libby Prison, Macon, Ga., and photos.
Deposited by the Naval Historical Foundation, 1964.

Bingham, Donald Cameron,　1882–1946
Papers, 1835–1932. 100 items.
Naval officer. Correspondence (1917–18) with Wilfred A. Edgerton and Hugh Rodman; comments of Herbert F. Leary, Ernest G. Small, and Alfred P. H. Tawresey concerning winter maneuvers of the U.S. Fleet (1929); general orders; notebooks; and speeches of Bingham and Dudley W. Knox.
Deposited by the Naval Historical Foundation, 1964.

Blake, Charles Follen,　1841–1879
Journal, 1862–64. 1 v. (156 p.)
Naval officer. Blake's personal journal describing his duty at the U.S. Naval Academy, cities he visited in Portugal, Spain, and Italy, and the blockade of Port Royal, S.C.
Deposited by the Naval Historical Foundation, 1958.

Bloch, Claude Charles,　1878–1967
Papers, 1926-44. 1400 items.

Naval officer. General correspondence, journal (1934) kept by Bloch as Judge Advocate General, U.S. Navy, subject file and miscellaneous materials, relating chiefly to Bloch's activities as commander in chief of the U.S. Fleet (1938) and commandant of the 14th Naval District, Pearl Harbor (1940–42.) Correspondents include Charles Edison, James Forrestal, Ernest Lee Jahncke, Hiram W. Johnson, Frank Knox, William D. Leahy, Chester W. Nimitz, David Sarnoff, Harold R. Stark, Claude A. Swanson, Burton K. Wheeler, and Harry H. Woodring.

Register published by the Library in 1973.

Deposited by the Naval Historical Foundation, 1968.

Boarman, Charles, 1795–1879

Letterbook, 1938–58, 1 v. (ca. 350 p.)

Naval officer. Letterbook kept by Boarman on the U.S.S. Fairfield and U.S.F. Brandywine and at the U.S. Navy Yard, New York. Includes correspondence, general orders, circulars, and specifications of charges for courts-martial. Correspondents include Benjamin F. Bache, Henry E. Ballard, George Bancroft, John Y. Mason, John B. Nicolson, James K. Paulding, Franklin Pierce, John Rodgers, Winfield Scott, Joseph Smith, and Levi Woodbury.

Deposited by the Naval Historical Foundation, 1963.

Bowen, Harold Gardiner, 1883–1965

Papers, 1931–65. 400 items.

Naval engineer. General correspondence, speech, article, and book file, photos, and printed matter, relating to Bowen's activities as director of the Naval Research Laboratory during World War II. The development of radar was carried out under his direction. Includes material on the Newcomen Society, a copy of Bowen's book The Edison Effect (1961), and reviews of his autobiography, Ships, Machinery and Mossbacks (1954). Correspondents include Karl T. Compton, William S. Dix, Ross Gunn, H. Struve Hensel, Donald L. Herr, Bart Nanus, Adlai E. Stevenson, Lewis L. Strauss, and James H. Wakelin.

Deposited by the Naval Historical Foundation, 1968.

Breck family

Papers, 1780–1949. 10 items.

Photocopies.

Letters concerning the transfer of cargo and a bill of sale for goods belonging to the ship Philippa (1780–83); and a genealogical table of the Breck family (1949).

Deposited by the Naval Historical Foundation, 1949.

Brent, Joseph Lancaster, 1826–1905
  Collection, 1863. 2 items.
  Confederate Army officer. Letter of Brent to Carter Littlepage Stevenson (1817–1888), Confederate Army officer, concerning the capture of the U.S.S. Indianola; and a steel engraving of Brent.
  Deposited by the Naval Historical Foundation, 1964

Bristol, Mark Lambert, 1868–1939
  Papers, 1913–18. 100 items.
  Naval officer. Carbon copies of letters sent, a speech, testimony before Congress, reports, memoranda, and a list of officers, relating to the naval aeronautics program, which Bristol served as director. Recipients of letters were Washington I. Chambers, Alan C. Hawley, Thomas S. Martin, Henry C. Mustin, and Henry Woodhouse.
  Deposited by the Naval Historical Foundation, 1964.

Browne, John Mills, 1831–1894
  Papers, 1853–78. 10 items.
  Naval surgeon. Letters of commendation from David G. Farragut and others, and five commissions.
  Deposited by the Naval Historical Foundation, 1949.

Browning family
  Papers, 1824–1917. 900 items.
  Family and official correspondence, journals, biographical file, genealogical and other notes, newspaper clippings, and printed matter, chiefly 1835–55, of Robert Lewright Browning (1803–1850), naval officer, his wife, Eleanor Hanlon Browning (1809–1857), and their sons, Robert Lewright Browning (1835–1860), marine officer, and Charles Henry Browning (1846–1926), genealogist. The journal includes material relating to voyages of the U.S.S. Vincennes, the U.S.S. Ohio, and the U.S.S. Congress, notes on the South Sea Islands, descriptions of Mediterranean and South American countries, watercolors of Turks, obituaries of naval officers, observations on the U.S. Navy, and diagrams and studies of Napoleon's campaigns, the bombardment of Odessa, 1854, and the attack on San Juan de Ulúa, 1838. Correspondents of Robert L. Browning, Sr., include Richard Bache, Caleb Cushing, Samuel F. Du Pont, William Sinclair, and Thomas D. Sumpter.
  Finding aid in the Library.
  Deposited by the Naval Historical Foundation, 1964.

Burns, Otway, 1775–1850
  Petition, 1813. 1 item.

Shipbuilder and privateer. Holograph petition (July 1, 1813) of Burns to James Monroe, Secretary of State, to obtain a letter of marque and reprisal for the schooner, Snap Dragon, New Bern, N.C.
Deposited by the Naval Historical Foundation, 1964.

Byrne, Edmund, d. 1850
Papers, 1825–50. 33 items.
Naval officer. Official correspondence, orders to duty, and commissions. Includes orders for Byrne, who was commanding the U.S.S. Decatur, to cruise the West Coast of Africa.
Deposited by the Naval Historical Foundation, 1949.

Callan, John Lansing, 1886–1958
Papers, 1907–56. 4000 items.
Aviator, aviation businessman, and naval officer. Correspondence, diaries, notebooks, orders to duty, subject file, awards, biographical file, speeches, articles, newspaper clippings, and printed matter, relating to personal and business interests, Callan's service with the Navy in World War I in France and Italy, activities during World War II as a prisoner of war in Italy, other World War II activities, his services at the Paris Peace Conference, and the Bikini atomic bomb tests in 1946. Correspondents include Nicholas Alexeyef, Richard E. Byrd, Jr., Benedict Crowell, James Doolittle, Beckwith Havens, J. C. Hunsaker, Rudolph E. Schoenfelt, Clara Studer, Juan Trippe, Peter Paul Vucetic, and Jay White.
Register published by the Library in 1968.
Deposited by the Naval Historical Foundation, 1959, 1962.

Canaga, Alfred Bruce, d. 1903
Commissions of Alfred Bruce Canaga and his son, Bruce Livingston Canaga, 1872–1928. 9 items.
Naval officers. Ten commissions, 1872–1903, of Alfred Bruce Canaga and nine commissions, 1905–28, of Bruce Livingston Canaga (1882–1966).
Deposited by the Naval Historical Foundation, 1950.

Caperton, William Banks, 1855–1941
Papers, 1873–1937. 700 items.
Naval officer. Correspondence (1913–35) largely with William S. Benson, reports (1915–16) to Josephus Daniels and Woodrow Wilson, orders to duty (1873–1919), and newspaper clippings (1913–37). Primary subject is Caperton's command of the cruiser squadron detailed to restore order in Haiti, 1915–16.
Deposited by the Naval Historical Foundation, 1968.

Carlin, James William, d. 1899
Letter, 1889. 1 item.
Naval officer. Letter (Mar. 26, 1889) to Mrs. Fuller describing the hurricane in Apia, Samoa, which destroyed the U.S.S. Vandalia and other ships and killed 50 American men.
Deposited by the Naval Historical Foundation, 1964.

Carpenter, Dudley Newcomb, b. 1874–
Papers, 1897–1901. 17 items.
Naval surgeon. Journal kept by Carpenter on board the U.S.S. Raleigh and the U.S.S. Olympia, three letters, newspaper clippings, and printed matter. Journal includes information concerning the Battle of Manila Bay and descriptions of Ceylon, Singapore, and cities on the Mediterranean Sea.
Deposited by the Naval Historical Foundation, 1950.

Carter, Samuel Powhatan, 1819–1891
Papers, 1882. 1 item.
Army officer during the Civil War and naval officer. Biographical material entitled "A Sketch of the Military Services of Sam. P. Carter, Brig. Genl. & Brevt. Maj. Genl. of [the] U.S. Vols. during the Rebellion of the Southern States, 1861–5," describing Carter's services with the Union forces in Kentucky, North Carolina, and Tennessee.
Deposited by the Naval Historical Foundation, 1949.

Cary, Clarence
Report, 1905, 1926. 1 item.
Confederate midshipman. Report prepared by Cary in 1905 for the State Dept. Library concerning the diary he had kept of his experiences and observations on board the C.S.S. Chickamauga, 1863–65, which had subsequently been used in the discussion of the Alabama Claims at the Geneva Tribunal. Written as a supplement to the diary, the report concludes with notes by James Parker and George W. Tennant in 1905 and by James Morris Morgan in 1926.
Deposited by the Naval Historical Foundation, 1964.

Casey, Silas, 1841–1913
Papers, 1771–1941. 300 items.
Naval officer. Correspondence, journal, daybook, bills, receipts, commissions, and other papers (chiefly 1862–1903) relating to Casey's naval service in Japan, the Civil War, the North Atlantic Squadron, Kanghoa Island, Korea, Samoa, Panama Bay, and the United States. Ships represented include the Colorado, Niagara, Portsmouth, Quinnebaug, Wisconsin, and Wyoming. Includes Joseph Coggeshall's account book of the privateers

Greenwich (1776), Marlborough (1777), and Providence.
Register published by the Library in 1968.
Deposited by the Naval Historical Foundation, 1949.

Chambers, Washington Irving, 1856–1934
Papers, 1871–1943. 12,000 items.

Naval officer. Correspondence, subject files, logbooks, memoranda, blueprints, photos, printed matter, and other papers relating to Chamber's service aboard the Pensacola and Portsmouth, with the Adolphus Washington Greely relief expedition (1884) to the Arctic, with the Nicaraguan Canal Survey Expedition (1884-85), at the Newport Torpedo Station, the New York Navy Yard, and in various administrative offices of the Navy Dept. The post–1910 material relates chiefly to Chambers' assignment (1910) to report on the development and application of aviation to naval forces and to dirigibles, helicopters, balloons, parachutes, and flight science and procedures. Correspondents include Thomas Scott Baldwin, W. Starling Burgess, Glenn Hammond Curtiss, Theodore G. Ellyson, Eugene Ely, Louis Godard, Roy Knabenshue, Grover Cleveland Loening, Glenn L. Martin, James Means, Holden Chester Richardson, John Rodgers, and John Henry Towers.

Described in Washington Irving Chambers: a register of his papers in in the Library of Congress (1967).
Deposited by the Naval Historical Foundation, 1954–69.

Chase, Philander, 1798–1824
Journal, 1818–19. 1 v. (207 p.)
Transcript (typewritten)

Naval chaplain. Typescript copy of a journal kept by Chase on the U.S.F. Guerrière containing descriptions of Copenhagen, St. Petersburg, Sicily, English villages, and the English countryside, with comparisons of the various cities and their customs. The journal also includes descriptions of the antiquities of Pompeii and Herculaneum, and a discussion of naval discipline on the American frigate.
Deposited by the Naval Historical Foundation, 1950.

Chester, Colby Mitchell, 1844–1932
Papers, 1913–28. 300 items.

Naval officer. Correspondence, research notes, and unpublished MSS., chiefly 1913–17, relating to Chester's study of Commodore Dudley Saltonstall and the Penobscot Bay Expedition in 1779.
Register published by the Library in 1973.
Deposited by the Naval Historical Foundation, 1964.

Cilley, Greenleaf,   1829–1899
Notebook, ca. 1847–67. 1 item.
Naval officer. Notebook containing instructions concerning cables, anchors, sail, and questions in navigation and astronomy. There are some diary observations made in August, no year given, of the Indians who lived near Puget Sound.
Deposited by the Naval Historical Foundation, 1949.

Clark, William Bell,   1889–1968
Collection, 1770–1950. 170 items.
In part, photocopies.
Naval historian. Material relating to the American Revolution, including logs from H.M.S. Fovey (1776), H.M.S. Kingfisher (1776), H.M.S. Liverpool (1776), H.M.S. Roebuck (1776), and the continental schooner Wasp (1776); letters (1770–80) of Benjamin Franklin; papers (1777) of the continental brig Lexington; John Young papers (1777–94); copies of letters, newspaper clippings, and orders, 1775–77. Also a speech and an article written by Clark.
Deposited by the Naval Historical Foundation, 1954 and 1964.

Claxton, Alexander,   ca. 1790–1841
Collection, 1832–41. 11 items.
Naval officer. Personal correspondence, including 9 letters of Claxton to Francis Sorrel concerning personal and family matters and political affairs of the Jackson period.
Deposited by the Naval Historical Foundation, 1949.

Cochrane, Alexander Forrester Inglis, 1758–1832
Letter, Sept. 3, 1814. 2 items.
Photocopy and transcript.
British admiral. Letter of Cochrane from Patuxent River, Chesapeake Bay, to William Frederick, Duke of Gloucester, giving an account of the results of the British attack on Washington, D. C.: U.S. flotilla destroyed, U.S. Army defeated, and the Capitol, President's house, and naval dockyard burned.
Deposited by the Naval Historical Foundation, 1961.

Cohen, Albert Morris,   1883–1959
Papers, 1904–55. 200 items.
Naval officer. Family and general correspondence, journals, reports, circulars, photos, and scrapbooks, relating to Cohen's services with the U.S. Naval Aviation Forces during World War I, and to his duties aboard the U.S.S. George Washington and the U.S.S. Louisiana. Family correspondents

include Cohen's father, Charles J. Cohen, his mother, Clotilda Florance Cohen, his brother, Henry Barnet Cohen, and his sister, Eleanor C. Hillman.
Deposited by the Naval Historical Foundation, 1968–69.

Colhoun, Edmund Ross,   1821–1897
Papers, 1839–88. 1200 items.
Naval officer. Correspondence, journals, and notebooks, relating to service aboard the U.S.S. Hartford as commander of the Asiatic fleet and including a few observations on American diplomacy and naval strength in the Far East.
Register published by the Library in 1967.
Deposited by the Naval Historical Foundation, 1950.

Conrad, Daniel B.,   d. 1869
Diaries, 1855–64. 2 v.
Naval officer and surgeon. Diaries in which Conrad records his service on the U.S.F. Congress and describes ports in the Mediterranean Sea. In the second diary Conrad also relates his refusal to take the oath of allegiance to the U.S. in 1861, his desertion from the U.S. Navy, and his subsequent service in the Confederate Navy.
Deposited by the Naval Historical Foundation, 1964.

Constitution (U.S.F.)
Collection, 1802–1955. 45 items.
In part, transcripts.
Correspondence, portion of a logbook, plans and specifications, payroll for repairs signed by Isaac Hull (1802), photos, and printed matter relating to the U.S.F. Constitution. Includes material collected by James A. Callan relating to the building of the frigate and material collected by C. M. Simners relating to the frigate's renovation.
Deposited by the Naval Historical Foundation, 1961.

Converse, George Albert,   1844–1909
Papers, 1895–1908. 250 items.
Naval officer. Letterbooks, general correspondence, printed matter, and miscellaneous material. Letterbooks contain copies of letters to Charles J. Bonaparte, Willard H. Brownson, French E. Chadwick, George Dewey, William F. Halsey, Henry Cabot Lodge, Benjamin R. Tillman, and George P. Wetmore, and are concerned primarily with naval topics, such as torpedo boats, battleships and the Russo-Japanese War (1904), and plans for the review of the Atlantic Fleet (1906).
Deposited by the Naval Historical Foundation, 1968.

Cook, John A.,   d. 1834
  Papers, 1812–31. 8 items.
  Naval officer. Correspondence, logbook kept on board the U.S.S. Fox together with financial notes, copy of A New Atlas of the World (1822) by Jedidiah and Sidney E. Morse, and commission signed by James Madison. Correspondents include Benjamin Cooper, Benjamin W. Crowninshield, Isaac Hull, Otho Norris, Benjamin Thomas, Thomas Tingey, and Melancthon T. Woolsey.
  Deposited by the Naval Historical Foundation, 1964.

Cooke, Harold David,   1879–1958
  Notebooks, 1918–45. 2 items.
  Transcripts (typewritten)
  Naval officer. Notebook containing correspondence relating to experiences in World Wars I and II, and notebook with Cooke's recollections of life in the Navy. Correspondents include Daniel M. Coffin and Donald John Munro.
  Deposited by the Naval Historical Foundation, 1964.

Cotton, Charles Stanhope,   1843–1909
  Papers, 1860–1921. 600 items.
  Naval officer. Official correspondence, newspaper clippings, invitations, and miscellaneous material, relating primarily to Cotton's command of the U.S.S. Harvard during the Spanish-American War, and to his activities as commander in chief of the U.S. Fleet (1903–04). Includes a few letters of the Civil War period. Correspondents include William S. Cowles, Charles H. Darling, Edwin Denby, David G. Farragut, William E. Harvey, and William H. Moody.
  Deposited by the Naval Historical Foundation, 1967.

Couthouy, Joseph Pitty,   1808–1864
  Correspondence, 1842. 3 items.
  Scientist. Business letters from A. O. Dayton and Thomas A. Smith.
  Deposited by the Naval Historical Foundation, 1964.

Crosby, Allyn J.,   1874–1955
  Papers, 1794–1940. 61 items.
  In part, photocopies.
  Historian. Correspondence and notes relating to Crosby's interest in the U.S.F. Constellation, a logbook (1799–1800) from the frigate, MS. of an unpublished article by Crosby entitled Constellation and L'Insurgente, and a map of the West Indies with a diagram of the battle of the U.S.F. Constellation and the French frigate Vengeance. Correspondents include Henry D. Cooke, John Masefield, William L. Rodgers, Elliot Snow, and

Walter Muir Whitehill.
Deposited by the Naval Historical Foundation, 1951 and 1960.

Cushing, Leonard F.,   1901–1962
Papers, 1794–1959. 3600 items.
Naval architect. Correspondence, blueprints, newspaper clippings, and photos, chiefly 1926–54, relating to the restoration of the U.S. Frigate Constitution and the U.S. Frigate Constellation. Includes material concerning the controversy over the authenticity of the Constellation.
Register published by the Library in 1969.
Deposited by the Naval Historical Foundation, 1963.

Dabney, John Bass,   d. 1826
Letter, 1814. 1 item.
Transcript.
U.S. consul at Fayal, Azore Islands. Letter to James Monroe, Secretary of State, reporting British violation of the neutrality of the port of Fayal, by attacking and destroying the American privateer, General Armstrong.
Deposited by the Naval Historical Foundation, 1964.

Dahlgren, John Adolphus Bernard,   1809–1870
Papers, 1843–70. 75 items.
Naval officer. Family correspondence, consisting primarily of letters from Dahlgren on board the U.S.F. Cumberland in the Mediterranean (1843–45) to his wife, Mary (Bunker) Dahlgren, describing places, persons, and social events. Includes letters of his daughter Eva Dahlgren, and of his second wife, Sarah Madeleine (Vinton) Dahlgren.
Deposited by the Naval Historical Foundation, 1964.

Danforth, Herbert L.,   1913–1973
Papers, 1942–72. 7 items.
Naval officer. Logbook (Dec. 29, 1942–July 14, 1943, with additional notes on June 6, 1972) kept on board the U.S.S. Pocahontas prior to and during the invasion (July 10, 1943) of Italy. Logbook entries provide information on the course of the battle and maneuvers on board ship, followed by a résumé evaluating the success of the mission, special citations for crew members, and deficiencies in training and equipment. Includes typewritten orders and general instructions for the crew.
Deposited by the Naval Historical Foundation, 1972.

De Haven, Edwin Jesse,   1816–1865
Papers, 1843–54. 15 items.
Naval officer. Correspondence; diaries, including one kept on board the

U.S.S. Truxton during an 1843 Mediterranean cruise and two for the period 1850–51 which present a detailed account of being caught and trapped in the ice of the Arctic seas; excerpts from William Parker Snow's "Journal in the Arctic Seas"; a photo of De Haven; and scrapbook and newspaper clippings concerning De Haven's command of an expedition to search the Arctic regions for Sir John Franklin, an explorer who had disappeared in 1845. During the search, De Haven discovered Grinnell Land. Correspondents include Robert R. Carter, William A. Graham, and John P. Kennedy.

Deposited by the Naval Historical Foundation, 1964.

Decatur, Stephen, 1752–1808

Papers, 1800–01. 3 items.

Photocopies.

Naval officer. Journal (334 p.) kept on board the U.S.F. Philadelphia, stationed at Guadeloupe; and photos of Decatur's daughter, Ann (Decatur) McKnight, and her husband, James McKnight.

Deposited by the Naval Historical Foundation, 1964.

Denig, Robert Gracy, d. 1924

Papers, 1885–87. 13 items.

Naval officer. Typed article by Denig entitled Reminiscences of the Cruise of the U.S.S. Brooklyn, describing his travels in Persia, and sketches of Persia by Charles Johnston Badger (1853–1932).

Deposited by the Naval Historical Foundation, 1964.

Dent, John Herbert, 1782–1823

Letterbook, 1803–10. 1 v. (ca. 50 p.)

Naval officer. Letterbook kept by Capt. Dent aboard the U.S.F. Constitution (1803–07) and the U.S.S. John Adams (1810). Correspondents include Samuel Barron, Hugh G. Campbell, Paul Hamilton, Edward Preble, and John Rodgers.

Deposited by the Naval Historical Foundation, 1964.

Dewey, George, 1837–1917

Papers, 1890–1943. 14 items.

Naval officer. Letter (Dec. 1, 1890) of Dewey to the commanding officer, U.S.S. Pinta, Sitka, Alaska; letter (undated) of Dewey to William Corcoran Hill; letter (May 10, 1898) of Charles A. Boutelle to Sally Phenix Hill with enclosed letter of Garret A. Hobart; historical account entitled Admiral Dewey and the Manila Campaign, compiled by Nathan Sargent, with a covering note by George G. Dewey, 1943; and photos.

Deposited by the Naval Historical Foundation, 1964.

Dickins, Francis William,   1844–1910
Collection, 1788–1905. 8 items.
Naval officer. Courts-martial of Jason Chamberlain and John Brazier, commission of Jonathan Bates, draft statement concerning growth of U.S. naval power and an errata communication to the Secretary of the Navy from John Rodgers, bill to render permanent the Naval Peace Establishment of the United States, and miscellaneous letters.
Deposited by the Naval Historical Foundation, 1970.

Dillen, Roscoe Franklin,   1881–1946
Papers, 1925–27. 45 items.
Naval officer. Reports on military and political conditions in China prepared by Dillen while commander of the U.S.S. Asheville, part of the Asiatic Fleet stationed at Tientsin, China, and a memorandum prepared by Dillen for the director of the U.S. Army War College on Negotiations Leading Up to the Building of the Panama Canal.
Deposited by the Naval Historical Foundation, 1969.

Dorn, Edward John,   1854–1937
Papers, 1868–1936. 1000 items.
Naval officer. Correspondence, diaries, orders to duty, speeches, notes on Guam and Samoa, photos, and printed matter, chiefly 1875–1922. Principal subjects include Dorn's cruises to Brazil, South Africa, Samoa, Guam, and Japan, and his problems as Governor of Samoa and Guam, especially in regard to missionaries, schools, water supply, and immigrants. Correspondents include Josephus Daniels, George Leland Dyer, Lloyd S. Shepley, Benjamin F. Tilley, and Beekman Winthrop.
Finding aid in the Library.
Deposited by the Naval Historical Foundation, 1969.

Dorsett, Edward Lee,   1883–
Collection, 1814–1926. 150 items.
Collector of naval history. Correspondence, congressional bills and reports relating to the U.S. Navy, photos of the specifications for the U.S.F. Constitution, and printed matter concerning John Paul Jones, the Battle of Lake Erie, and the history of the U.S. Navy.
Finding aid in the Library.
Deposited by the Naval Historical Foundation, 1964.

Dow, Leonard James,   1902–1967
Papers, 1945–67. 2500 items.
Naval officer. Correspondence, subject file, speech and article file, and miscellaneous material, chiefly 1956–63, relating primarily to Dow's post-

retirement career as consultant in civil defense, antisubmarine warfare, and communications for government and private industry. Correspondents include Robert B. Carney, William F. Halsey, John T. Hayward, Noel B. McLean, William K. Mendenhall, Gilven M. Slonim, Lloyd P. Smith, Harold E. Stassen, and Ronald A. Veeder.

Finding aid in the Library.

Deposited by the Naval Historical Foundation, 1967.

Dulany, Bladen, 1792–1856

Papers, 1817–55. 500 items.

Naval officer. Correspondence, journals, orders to duty, bills, receipts, inventories, and printed matter, chiefly relating to Dulany's tour of duty (1852–55) as commander of the South Pacific Squadron. Correspondents include Augustus L. Case, J. Randolph Clay, Edmund R. Colhoun, William M. Crane, Jefferson Davis, Thomas A. Dornin, William A. Graham, William Harris, William W. Hunter, John P. Kennedy, William D. Salter, Luther Severance, Solomon P. Sharp, William Sinclair, Thomas W. Ward, Philo White, and John B. Williams.

Register published by the Library in 1970.

Deposited by the Naval Historical Foundation, 1949.

Dungan, William W., 1836–1904

Collection, 1862–97. 11 items.

Naval officer. Orders to duty, 1862–97.

Deposited by the Naval Historical Foundation.

Emory, William Hemsley, 1846–1917

Papers, 1877–1948. 2100 items.

Naval officer. Correspondence, journal, conduct and rating books, photos, and printed matter, chiefly 1894–1906, relating to Emory's experience commanding the U.S.S. Yosemite during the Spanish-American War. Correspondents include George W. Coffin, John D. Long, Cyrus E. Lothrop and Truman H. Newberry.

Finding aid in the Library.

Deposited by the Naval Historical Foundation, 1964.

Evans, Robley Dunglison, 1846–1912

Papers, 1901–50. 5 items.

Naval officer. Typescript, in bound volume, of Sea Fight at Santiago as Seen from the Iowa, with pictures of Evans and autographs of William McKinley, Theodore Roosevelt, Andrew S. Rowan, and William T. Sampson; photo of Evans (1901); printed matter; and two copies of letters concerning the collection. Evans participated in the Civil War and later com-

manded the U.S.S. Iowa, engaging in the battle with Cervera's fleet, 1898.
Deposited by the Naval Historical Foundation, 1964.

Farragut, David Glasgow,   1801–1870
Papers, 1816–69. 400 items.
Naval officer. Correspondence (including letterbooks), biographical file,
invitations, and other material, chiefly 1834–60, relating primarily to
Farragut's naval activities, especially his role in the protection of American
interests in Mexico during the pre-Civil War period. Includes letters to
Farragut from Charles Folsom and copies of letters from Farragut to James
Barron, Charles Baudin, Alexander J. Dallas, John A. Dahlgren, Lyman
Copeland Draper, Duncan N. Ingraham, William D. Jones, John Lenthall,
Stephen R. Mallory, Matthew F. Maury, Charles Morris, James K. Paulding,
Antonio López de Santa Anna, and Isaac Toucey.
Finding aid in the Library.
Deposited by the Naval Historical Foundation, 1969.

Fentress, Walter E. H.
Literary manuscript, 1876. 1 item (45 p.)
Naval officer. Typescript of Fentress' book 1775.1875. [sic] Centennial
History of the United States Navy Yard at Portsmouth, N.H. (1876).
Deposited by the Naval Historical Foundation, 1964.

Fillebrown, Thomas Scott,   1834–1884
Letter, 1861. 1 item.
Naval officer. Holograph letter (Nov. 16, 1861) of Fillebrown, on board
the U.S.S. Roanoke, Old Point Comfort, Va., to Samuel Heintzelman,
discussing war news, including the arrival of troops from Massachusetts
and Connecticut, the anticipated attack by the C.S.S. Merrimack, and Capt.
Charles Wilkes' capture of John Slidell and James M. Mason (the "Trent
affair").
Deposited by the Naval Historical Foundation, 1964.

Flirt (U.S.S.)
Journal, Sept. 1841-June 1842. 1 v. (ca. 150 p.)
Journal kept on board the U.S. Schooner Flirt, commanded by John T.
McLaughlin. Entries relate principally to observations on weather and the
sea, shipboard routine, and discipline, during the period of its cruise in the
waters of Florida and Cuba.
Deposited by the Naval Historical Foundation, 1964.

Foulk, George Clayton,   1856–1893
Papers, 1872–1950. 300 items.

In part, transcripts (typewritten)

Naval officer. Correspondence (1872–1917) chiefly concerning Foulk's personal life and his mission in Korea, notebook (1884) kept on board the U.S.S. Trenton describing burial practices in Bombay, invitations (1885) to attend palace functions in Korea, newspaper clippings (1883–93), envelopes with notations, and cards and slips (ca. 1950) identifying publications on Korea.

Deposited by the Naval Historical Foundation, 1969.

Fox, Josiah,   1763–1847
Papers, 1795–1845. 15 items.

Naval constructor. General correspondence and miscellany concerned primarily with Fox's appointment as naval constructor in 1798, the revocation of that appointment in 1801, his appointment as head ship carpenter and naval constructor, and the subsequent revocation of that appointment four years later.

Deposited by the Naval Historical Foundation, 1955.

Fullam, William Freeland,   1855–1926
Papers, 1877–1919. 3850 items.

Naval officer and columnist. Correspondence, bulletins, biographical data, Navy newssheets, radio dispatches, reports, orders, commissions, transcripts of congressional testimony, drafts of Fullam's writings, photos, clippings and other records called historical war diaries. The material relates to Fullam's interest in Navy administrative reorganization, the development of naval aviation, his service off the coast of Cuba during the Spanish-American War, and tours of duty in the West Indies and Caribbean waters (1904–14) aboard the gunboat Marietta. Correspondents include William Shepherd Benson, William E. Borah, Josephus Daniels, William "Billy" Mitchell, and Madame Ernestine Schumann-Heink.

Register published by the Library in 1973.

Deposited by the Naval Historical Foundation, 1952.

Furer, Julius Augustus,   1880–1963
Papers, 1910–62. 2800 items.

Naval officer. Correspondence; diary (1941–45); subject file; speech, article, and book file, including numerous articles on naval and maritime subjects, published in the Encyclopedia Americana; and miscellaneous material, chiefly 1915–61, relating to Furer's activities as director of the salvaging of the submarine U.S.S. F–4, as assistant naval attaché at London, as secretary of the U.S. Naval Academy's class of 1901, and as coordinator of naval research and development. Correspondents include Arleigh Burke, Vannevar Bush, Karl T. Compton, John Foster Dulles, Ernest M. Eller,

Albert Furer, Kurt Fürer, William F. Halsey, John B. Heffernan, Jerome C. Hunsaker, Dudley W. Knox, Charles Little, Samuel E. Morison, and Clifton Toal.

Register published by the Library in 1973.

Deposited by the Naval Historical Foundation, 1968.

Furman, Greene Chandler
Collection, 1862–1954. 3 items.
Photocopies.

Lawyer. Letter (Mar. 13, 1862) of Henry Marshall to Dr. S. C. Furman concerning the Confederate Congress; letter (Dec. 9, 1863) of D. E. C. Kemper to Henry Marshall concerning the court-martial of Kemper's brother; and letter (Jan. 21, 1954) of Greene C. Furman to John B. Heffernan explaining the letters of 1862 and 1863.

Deposited by the Naval Historical Foundation, 1964.

Fyffe, Joseph P., 1832–1896
Letter, 1892. 1 item.
Transcript.

Naval officer. Satirical report written by Fyffe to the chief of the Bureau of Yards and Docks.

Deposited by the Naval Historical Foundation, 1964.

Gantt, Benjamin S., d. 1852
Papers, 1834–51. 6 items.

Naval officer. Official and personal journals kept by Gantt on board the U.S.S. St. Louis, U.S.S. Independence, U.S.S. Fairfield, and other ships in the Caribbean, European, and South American Squadrons. Personal journals contain notes, verse, and descriptions of the countries visited.

Deposited by the Naval Historical Foundation, 1950.

Gardner, Obed
Will, 1841. 1 item.
Transcript (typewritten)

Master mariner. Typescript of Gardner's will, May 30, 1841, Siasconset, Mass. (Nantucket Island).

Deposited by the Naval Historical Foundation, 1964.

Gill, Charles Clifford, 1885–1948
Papers, 1916–35. 3 items.

Naval officer. Two typewritten unpublished articles entitled Escape of Goeben and Breslau and The Battle of Jutland, and printed matter.

Deposited by the Naval Historical Foundation, 1950.

Gillett, Simon Palmer,   d. 1910
   Papers, 1858–76. 12 items.
   Naval officer. Correspondence, notebook, photos, and newspaper clipping.
Includes a letter from John Crittenden Watson and letters from Gillett to
his wife concerning his duty at Charleston, S.C., and the capture of Jeffer-
son Davis.
   Deposited by the Naval Historical Foundation, 1964.

Gillis, James H.,   1831–1910
   Collection, 1854–87. 5 items.
   Naval officer. Commissions for passed midshipman, lieutenant, com-
mander, captain, and commodore granted to Gillis.
   Deposited by the Naval Historical Foundation, 1964.

Gleaves, Albert,   1858–1937
   Papers, 1803–1946. 6000 items.
   Naval officer, author, and historian. Correspondence, diaries, journals,
speeches, articles, books, scrapbooks, reports of the Asiatic Fleet, notebooks,
photos, newspaper clippings, biographical material, poetry file, printed
matter, and miscellaneous papers, relating to Gleaves' naval career, torpedo
ordinance, his publications, especially the book James Lawrence (1904),
naval history, and his command of the Asiatic Fleet during which he showed
a talent for diplomacy in dealing with representatives of the Russian,
Chinese, and Japanese governments. Ships represented include the Alabama,
Cushing, Dolphin, and Mayflower. Correspondents include H. A. Baldridge,
W. E. Beard, William Shepherd Benson, Edward G. Blakeslee, J. C. Breckin-
ridge, Josephus Daniels, Charles E. Fox, Hilary P. Jones, Dudley Wright
Knox, Frank K. Polk, George Haven Putnam, Raymond P. Rodgers, David
F. Sellers, Joshua Slocum, Clifford H. West, and Spencer J. Wood.
   Register published by the Library in 1968.
   Deposited by the Naval Historical Foundation, 1950, 1955.

Gove family
   Papers of Jesse Augustus Gove (1824–1862) and of his son, Charles
Augustus Gove (1854–1933), 1848–1911. 7 items.
   Correspondence of Jesse Augustus Gove, Army officer in the Mexican
War and the Civil War, including letters from Jefferson Davis and
Richard C. Drum; private journal describing battlefield experiences in the
Civil War until his death at the Battle of Chickahominy; and printed mat-
ter. Printed matter of Charles Augustus Gove, naval officer in the Spanish-
American War, relating to his command of the U.S.S. Delaware and an
invitation to attend the coronation of King George and Queen Mary, 1911.
   Deposited by the Naval Historical Foundation, 1964.

Grattan, John W.,   b. 1841
Papers, 1862–1937. 300 items.
Naval officer. Correspondence, journal, MSS. of writings, sketches, photos, and printed matter, chiefly 1862–63, relating to Grattan's Civil War experiences, including three months in the U.S. Army.
Deposited by the Naval Historical Foundation, 1949.

Green, Joseph F.,   b. 1811
Papers, 1828–1960. 60 items.
Naval officer. Primarily correspondence (1862–64) relating to Green's command of the U.S.S. Canandaigua, a part of the South Atlantic Blockading Squadron surrounding Charleston, S.C. Other material includes statements concerning Green's qualifications for promotion for service during the Civil War; instructions for the attack on Morrill's Inlet, S.C., 1863–64; report on the French attack on Vera Cruz, Mexico, 1838; and correspondence (1960) relating to the collection. Correspondents include James C. Chaplin, John J. Cornwell, John A. Dahlgren, Samuel F. Du Pont, Sylvanus W. Godon, Henry DeHaven Manley, Charles W. Pickering, and Henry C. Victor.
Deposited by the Naval Historical Foundation, 1960.

Greene, Albert S.,   1838–1896
Papers, 1853–96. 300 items.
Naval officer. Diary concerning the loss of the U.S.S. Wateree in an earthquake (1868) at Arica, Peru (now Arica, Chile); copies of Greene's letters, some requesting that naval engineers be granted the rank of line officers; orders to duty; reports on the loss of the U.S.S. Vandalia in a Samoan hurricane (1889); plates and diagrams, some relating to Greene's inventions; photos; and printed matter concerning the Military Order of the Loyal Legion.
Deposited by the Naval Historical Foundation, 1970.

Greenslade, John Wills,   1880–1950
Papers, 1937–57. 900 items.
In part, photocopies.
Naval officer. Official correspondence, reports, blueprints, dispatches, contracts, maps, charts, tables, memoranda, clippings, and aerial photos, chiefly 1940–41, relating to the establishment of military bases along the Atlantic coastline on British territory. Places represented include Antigua, the Bahamas, British Guiana, Jamaica, Martinique, Newfoundland, Santa Lucia, and Trinidad. Correspondents include Stanley Truman Brooks.
Deposited by the Naval Historical Foundation, 1968.

Griffin, Virgil Childers,   1891–1957
Flight records, 1916–46. 33 items.
Naval officer. Flight records, including nine aviator flight logbooks, documenting Griffin's service as a naval aviator at U.S. naval air stations and bases in Pensacola, Fla., Pearl Harbor, Hawaii, Newport, R.I., Anacostia, D.C., San Juan, Puerto Rico, and Norman, Okla.
Deposited by the Naval Historical Foundation, 1962.

Gwinn, John, 1791–1849
Papers, 1815–64. 900 items.
Naval officer. Official and general correspondence, personal journals, commissions, printed matter, and miscellaneous material, chiefly 1825–49, documenting the Navy's peacetime mission of protecting American interests and commerce at home and abroad. Includes material concerning the court-martial of Alexander Slidell MacKenzie, for which Gwinn served on the jury. Correspondents include William Bainbridge, George Bancroft, James Biddle, William C. Bolton, David Conner, William M. Crane, Benjamin Crowninshield, John Y. Mason, William Ballard Preston, Samuel L. Southard, Smith Thompson, Alexander Todd, and William Winthrop.
Finding aid in the Library.
Deposited by the Naval Historical Foundation, 1964.

Halsey, William Frederick,   1882–1959
Papers, 1907–59. 22,000 items.
In part, photocopies.
Naval officer. Correspondence, war diaries, narratives of military campaigns, military orders, yearbooks, charts, books, periodicals, poems, songs, newspaper clippings, and memorabilia, chiefly 1942–59, relating to Halsey's naval and business career, his personal life and club activities, and the history of U.S. naval involvement in the Pacific Theater during World War II. Includes correspondence with Chester W. Nimitz relating to personnel, shipping, duties of officers, battles, desirability of military locations, and personal interests.
Finding aid in the Library.
Deposited by the Naval Historical Foundation, 1972.

Harrington, Purnell Frederick,   1844–1937
Papers, 1861–85. 100 items.
Naval officer. Chiefly orders and official correspondence, supplemented by personnel and academic records, relating to Harrington's service as acting ensign on the U.S.S. Monongahela during the Civil War, and as commander of the U.S.S. Juniata during the Franco-Chinese War (1884–85). Includes a letter (Aug. 24, 1884) from William W. Cooper, Ningpo, China,

concerning protection of the lives and property of U.S. and British citizens.
Deposited by the Naval Historical Foundation, 1972.

Harrison, George W., 1823–1844

Papers, 1839–44. 39 items.

Naval officer. Correspondence, chiefly letters between Harrison and his
father, Thomas, and his mother, Sidney A. Harrison, and miscellaneous
material. Harrison's letters describe cities he visited in South America and
South Africa. There is also correspondence concerning his death in Macao.
Deposited by the Naval Historical Foundation, 1950.

Hatch, John Porter, 1822–1901

Letter, 1866. 1 item.

Transcript.

Army officer. Copy of a letter (Oct. 4, 1866) of Hatch to George Henry
Preble (1816–1885), U.S. naval officer, commending Preble's brigade for
meritorious service with the U.S. Army in the campaign in South Carolina,
1864–65.
Deposited by the Naval Historical Foundation, 1964.

Hooper, Stanford Caldwell, 1884–1955

Papers, 1899–1955. 14,000 items.

Naval officer and electronics consultant. Correspondence, diaries, tape
recordings, notebooks, financial and legal papers, research notes, speeches,
articles, bibliographical file, and newspaper clippings, relating to Hooper's
part in the planning and growth of radio communications in government
service, his work in building the shore-detection radio finder system for the
Navy, his design and construction of many of the Navy's high-power radio
stations, his delegacy to national and international radio conferences in the
1920's and 1930's, and his role in persuading the U.S. Government to help
establish the Radio Corporation of America. Other subjects include long-life
receiving and transmitting tubes, high-power vacuum tubes, simultaneous
multiwave communications systems, remote control radio operational
techniques, depth finders, sound-oscillated radio systems, the application
of long distance radio techniques to aircraft, submarine sound detection
systems, and radio-controlled target practice experiments. Correspondents
include William S. Benson, Mark L. Bristol, Richard E. Byrd, Jr., Royal
S. Copeland, Josephus Daniels, John Hays Hammond, Jr., James C.
Harbord, Hiram W. Johnson, Jr., Emory S. Land, Thomas A. Marshall,
Elihu Root, Daniel C. Roper, David Sarnoff, and Owen D. Young.
Register published by the Library in 1968.
Deposited by the Naval Historical Foundation, 1958–59.

Horne, Frederick Joseph, 1880–1959

Papers, 1908–67. 1000 items.

Naval officer. General correspondence (1919–65), speeches and articles (1922–46), congressional material (1943–59), flight logbooks (1931, 1933–37), minutes and reports (1945–46), and miscellany, documenting Horne's naval career, including his duties as Vice Chief of Naval Operations (1942). Correspondents include Clarence Darrow, Richard M. Nixon, and Robert C. Wilson.

Deposited by the Naval Historical Foundation, 1968.

Horner, Gustavus R. B., 1806–1892

Papers, 1826–1911. 4900 items.

Naval surgeon and author. Correspondence, daybooks, medical journals, MSS. of Horner's published books, registers of weather, and printed matter, chiefly 1840–70, and relating to the medical aspects of Horner's naval career. Correspondents include John Deering, Phineas J. Horwitz, Joseph B. Hull, and Robert Pettit.

Register published by the Library in 1970.

Deposited by the Naval Historical Foundation, 1950, 1963.

Independence (U.S.S.)

Order book, 1815. 1 item (44 p.)

Transcript (typewritten)

Order book of the U.S.S. Independence, commanded by William M. Crane. Orders relate to discipline on board ship.

Original on display, Holman and Lutz, Inc., Porland, Ore.

Deposited by the Naval Historical Foundation, 1964.

Johnson, Philip Carrigan, 1828–1887

Correspondence, May–June, 1861. 6 items.

Transcript (typewritten)

Naval officer. Correspondence with William Inman, commanding the U.S. African Squadron, concerning charges that the officers of the U.S.F. Constellation had been guilty of misconduct, and a letter to John Nicholas, commanding the U.S.F. Constellation, concerning Johnson's investigation on the Congo River of two American brigs, one of which appeared to be engaged in the slave trade.

Deposited by the Naval Historical Foundation, 1964.

Jones, Hilary Pollard, 1863–1938

Papers, 1889–1937. 2400 items.

Naval officer. Correspondence, orders to duty, speeches, and other material, chiefly 1920–30, and relating primarily to the Washington Conference on Disarmament, the London Naval Conference, the Presidential

Oil Commission, and the Naval Oil Reserves Commission. Correspondents include Colby M. Chester, Hugh Gibson, Joseph C. Grew, George West Holland, Frank B. Kellogg, Dudley W. Knox, John D. McDonald, George Otis Smith, Henry L. Stimson, Curtis D. Wilbur, and Harry Curran Wilbur. Finding aid in the Library.
Deposited by the Naval Historical Foundation, 1951, 1955, and 1969.

Jones, John Paul, 1747–1792
Certificate, 1785. 1 item.
Photocopy.
Naval officer, Continental Navy. Certificate signed by George Washington attesting Jones' membership in the Society of the Cincinnati.
Deposited by the Naval Historical Foundation, 1964.

Jones, P. A. J. P.
Papers, 1805–13. 15 items.
Naval officer. Regulations for the Delaware flotilla, commanded by Jones, specifications for a court-martial of H. H. Kennedy, and two newspapers.
Deposited by the Naval Historical Foundation, 1964.

Julian, Charles
Diary, 1897–99. 1 v. (80 p.)
Photocopy.
Naval officer. Diary kept by Julian on board the U.S.S. Vermont and U.S.S. Baltimore, recording daily shipboard events and describing in detail the Battle of Manila Bay.
Deposited by the Naval Historical Foundation, 1964.

Kaiser, Louis Anthony, 1870–1939
Diary, 1899–1901. 1 item.
Transcript (typewritten)
Naval officer. Diary kept by Kaiser while serving aboard the U.S.S. Concord in the Philippine Islands. Includes his observations on the Philippine Insurrection.
Deposited by the Naval Historical Foundation, 1949.

Kearny, Thomas, 1878–1942
Collection, 1931–36. 3 items.
Lawyer. Letters from Nelson Trusler Johnson and Edward C. Wynne and an article by Tingfu Fuller Tsiang concerning the opening of the ports of China by Lawrence Kearny in 1842–43.
Deposited by the Naval Historical Foundation, 1964.

Kellogg, Edward Nealy,   1841–1874
Papers of Edward Nealy Kellogg and Edward Stanley Kellogg, 1859–1937.
500 items.

Biographical data, commissions, orders to duty, and miscellaneous material, chiefly 1859–1919, relating to the naval careers of Edward Nealy Kellogg and his son, Edward Stanley Kellogg (1870–1948). Edward Nealy Kellogg's private journal contains notes, poems, drawings of ships and riggings, newspaper clippings, and pressed flora.

Finding aid in the Library.

Deposited by the Naval Historical Foundation, 1949 and 1964.

Kimberly, Louis Ashfield,   1830–1902
Papers, 1889–96. 50 items.

Naval officer. Article and sketches by Kimberly, printed matter, and charts relating to the Samoan hurricane in 1889; MS. articles by Kimberly entitled Our Navy, Reminiscence of [an] African Cruise, and Reminisence [sic] of My First Cruise to Japan, and an untitled article on Kimberly's first cruise as a midshipman.

Deposited by the Naval Historical Foundation, 1958.

Kimmel, Husband Edward,   1882–1968
Papers, 1954–55. 1 reel of microfilm (negative) 200 items.

Naval officer. Correspondence and newspaper and magazine articles relating to the publication of Kimmel's book Admiral Kimmel's Story (1955) concerning the controversy surrounding the attack on Pearl Harbor, Kimmel's defense of his position in that affair, and the role of Franklin D. Roosevelt. Correspondents include John O. Beaty, Joseph Grew, Fred L. Krause, H. Hayes Landon, Romaine Poindexter, James O. Richardson, John F. Shafroth, Edgar W. Waybright, and Harry E. Yarnell.

Deposited by the Naval Historical Foundation, 1957.

King, Ernest Joseph,   1878–1956
Papers, 1908–66. 10,000 items.

Naval officer. Official and general correspondence, orders to duty, speech, article, and book file, memoranda, notes, photos, printed matter, and miscellany, chiefly 1936–52, relating primarily to King's activities as commander in chief of the U.S. Fleet and Chief of Naval Operations during World War II, including his participation in all the Allied conferences from the Argentine Conference (Aug. 1941) to the Potsdam Conference (July 1945). Correspondents include Henry H. Arnold, Clement R. Attlee, Bernard M. Baruch, Omar N. Bradley, Mark Clark, Charles Edison, Dwight D. Eisenhower, Douglas Southall Freeman, William F. Halsey, Cordell Hull, Frank Knox, Paul W. Litchfield, Oliver Lyttleton, George Marshall, Louis Mountbatten, Chester W. Nimitz, Charles F. A. Portal, Franklin D. Roose-

velt, Dorothy Thompson, Harry S. Truman, and Orville Wright.
Finding aid in the Library.
Deposited by the Naval Historical Foundation, 1970–71.

Kingsley, Louis Albert, d. 1896
Papers, 1866–68. 2 items.
Naval officer. Station bills and official logbook, including a map of the Strait of Magellan, kept by Kingsley on the U.S.S. Lackawanna, Pacific Squadron.
Deposited by the Naval Historical Foundation, 1958, 1964.

Kirk, Alan Goodrich, 1888–1963
Papers, 1919–61. 125 items.
Naval officer and diplomat. General correspondence, orders to duty (1919–58), and miscellaneous material, relating primarily to Kirk's services as Ambassador to Belgium (1946), as a member of the United Nations Special Committee on the Balkans (1947–48), and as Ambassador to the U.S.S.R. (1948–52). Includes material relating to Kirk's trip to the Belgian Congo (1958) and to his activities as a member of the New York Civil Defense Commission (1956). Correspondents include Charles E. Bohlen, J. William Fulbright, and Kirk's son, William T. Kirk.
Deposited by the Naval Historical Foundation, 1968.

Knowles, Herbert Bain, 1894–
Papers, 1941–45. 1500 items.
In part, photocopies.
Naval officer. Correspondence, orders to duty, subject file concerning invasion plans and occupation reports for Guam, Japan, Kwajalein, Leyte, Lingayen, Okinawa, Saipan, and Tarawa, and printed matter, relating to Knowles' service with the Amphibious Forces in the Pacific (1942–45). Correspondents include James Forrestal, James L. Kauffman, and George R. Stone.
Deposited by the Naval Historical Foundation, 1968.

Knox, Dudley Wright, 1877–1960
Papers, ca. 1865–1950. 6500 items.
Naval officer and author. Correspondence, subject files, speeches, articles, book file, printed matter, newspaper clippings, and miscellaneous material, chiefly 1921–46, relating to Knox's many activities as director of the U.S. Office of Naval Records and Library (1921–46), as secretary of the Naval Historical Foundation (1926–46), and as author of books and articles on naval affairs. The papers document Knox's views on such subjects as international naval limitation conferences, naval aviation, the revival of a

strong merchant marine, naval preparedness, Far Eastern affairs, foreign trade, and national defense. Includes typescripts of Knox's book A History of the United States Navy (1936) and reviews, clippings, and letters concerning it. Correspondents include J. V. Babcock, Hanson W. Baldwin, Willard H. Brownson, George P. Colvocoresses, Bennett Cerf, William Bell Clark, Albert L. Cox, Josephus Daniels, H. A. De Weerd, George Edmund Foss, Thomas Goddard Frothingham, J. A. Furer, William Howard Gardiner, Edwin Grabhorn, Jan Hasbrouck, Hiram W. Johnson, Henry Cabot Lodge, William S. Sims, and Lewis L. Strauss.

Register published by the Library in 1971.

Deposited by the Naval Historical Foundation, 1953.

Konter, Richard Wesley, 1882–

Article, 1920. 1 item.

Chief electrician, U.S. Navy. Unpublished article by Konter entitled Wreck of the U.S.S. Charleston, concerning the sinking (1899) of the U.S.S. Charleston off Camiguin Island in the Philippines.

Deposited by the Naval Historical Foundation, 1960.

Lee, Samuel Phillips, 1812–1897

Papers, 1860–69. 19,000 items.

Naval officer. Correspondence, logbook abstracts, reports, lists, memoranda, requisition orders, and printed matter, relating to the naval activities of the Union forces in the Civil War, chiefly to Lee's service commanding the North Atlantic Blockading Squadron (1862–64) and the Mississippi Squadron (1864–65). Correspondents include J. B. Devoe, John G. Foster, the Navy Dept., and Gideon Welles, Secretary of the Navy.

Register published in 1967 by the Library.

Deposited by the Naval Historical Foundation, 1949.

Leonard, John Calvin, 1859–1937

Papers, 1887–1920. 300 items.

Naval officer. Twelve diaries relating to Leonard's naval career, the Navy's role in the Spanish-American War and World War I, and family matters; a testimonial (1913); and newspaper clippings (1898–99).

Finding aid in the Library.

Deposited by the Naval Historical Foundation, 1950.

Linnet (H.M.S.)

Collection, 1814. 12 items.

Photocopies.

Letters of Peter Fischer, captain, and William Drew, first lieutenant, H.M.S. Linnet; order book; and covers of an order book for H.M.S. Shan-

non, all relating to the battle of Lake Champlain (War of 1812).
Deposited by the Naval Historical Foundation, 1964.

Little, Charles G., 1895–
Papers, 1917–57. 78 items.
Naval officer. Correspondence, memoranda, data on dirigibles, telegrams,
and printed matter, relating to Little's career as an officer in the Naval Reserve Flying Corps. Includes Little's reports on his flights, his suggestions for
the future of naval aviation organization, and requisitions for supplies.
Deposited by the Naval Historical Foundation, 1958.

Lockwood, Charles Andrews, 1890–1967
Papers, 1904–67. 7600 items.
In part, photocopies.
Naval officer. Official and personal correspondence (1920–45), diaries
(1935–63), TSS. of Lockwood's books, military orders, speeches, articles,
and newspaper clippings. Subject file containing naval biographies, reports,
addresses, articles, log extracts, and lists of personnel of various naval vessels,
dating from World War II through Lockwood's retirement, and relating to
several aspects of submarine warfare, including its use by the Japanese, and
to wartime activities in the Pacific Theater. Includes diary of John Allison
Fitzgerald, prisoner of war in Japan.
Finding aid in the Library.
Deposited by the Naval Historical Foundation, 1972.

Lowe, John, 1838–1930
Papers, 1860–1945. 600 items.
Naval officer. Private journals; orders to duty; scrapbook containing
newspaper clippings, typewritten copies of articles, holograph notes, and
reprints of articles by Lowe; and miscellaneous material. The journals, some
of which have been edited by Lowe's daughter, Edith Blinston Lowe,
contain personal entries, entries pertaining to various ships, autograph
letters, copies of letters, general orders, circulars, newspaper clippings,
diagrams, photos, and printed matter. Among the correspondents in the
journals are Daniel Ammen and Aniceto G. Menocal in the journal kept
on the U.S.S. Despatch; Samuel S. Cox, William H. Emory, and Edwin
Thacher in the journal kept on the U.S.S. Dolphin and the U.S.S. Thetis;
and Philip Hichborn in the journal kept on the U.S.S. New York. The
journal kept on the submarine Holland contains copies of correspondence
with John D. Long. The bulk of the material is dated 1870–98.
Finding aid in the Library.
Deposited by the Naval Historical Foundation, 1964.

Luce, Stephen Bleecker, 1827–1917
  Papers, 1799–1938. 8000 items.
  Naval officer. Correspondence, journals, order books, subject files, scrap-books, notebooks, newspaper clippings, and miscellany, chiefly 1842–1912, documenting Luce's naval career, including his work to establish the U.S. Naval War College and the Naval Historical Society, his service with the South Atlantic Blockading Squadron (1863–65), and his diplomatic role in the arbitration of the Canadian fisheries dispute (1887). Correspondents include Nelson W. Aldrich, George E. Belknap, Charles J. Bonaparte, George Dewey, Albert Gleaves, Albert Bushnell Hart, Henry Cabot Lodge, Alfred T. Mahan, Theodore Roosevelt, John Sherman, William S. Sims, and William C. Whitney.
  Register published in 1969 by the Library.
  Deposited by the Naval Historical Foundation, 1950.

Lull, Edward Phelps, d. 1887
  Record book, 1867–79. 1 v. (68 p.)
  Naval officer. Record book kept by Lull as assistant professor of mathematics at the U.S. Naval Academy.
  Deposited by the Naval Historical Foundation, 1964.

Mahan, Alfred Thayer, 1840–1914
  Papers, 1861–1913. 5 items.
  Naval officer and author. Four letters (1911–13) of Mahan to Carter H. Fitz-Hugh concerning U.S. defense policy, the Panama Canal, and Germany's territorial conditions, and one letter (Oct. 10, 1861) to C. S. Newcome from the U.S. Steamer Pocahontas.
  Deposited by the Naval Historical Foundation, 1969.

Malvern (U.S.S.)
  Notebook, ca. 1863. 1 v. (ca. 50 p.)
  Notebook containing regulations for the crew of the U.S.S. Malvern.
  Deposited by the Naval Historical Foundation, 1964.

Manila Bay Society
  Records, 1901–33. 300 items.
  Correspondence, minutes, financial records, programs, and photos. Correspondents include William P. Biddle, Dudley N. Carpenter, George P. Colvocoresses, George Dewey, Mildred McLean Dewey, George B. Ransom, and John C. Wise.
  Deposited by the Naval Historical Foundation, 1950.

Marsh, Charles Carlton,   1858–1933
Papers, 1898–1917. 28 items.
Naval officer. Scrapbook with photos pertaining to the Spanish-American War and with clippings and photos pertaining to World War I.
Deposited by the Naval Historical Foundation, 1950.

Marshall, William Alexander,   1849–1926
Papers, 1876–1906. 100 items.
Naval officer. Official correspondence, personal diary, orders to duty, printed material, and photos, chiefly relating to Marshall's duty as commander of the U.S.S. Vicksburg in Korean waters in 1904 during the Russo-Japanese War. Correspondents include Horace Newton Allen and Edwin T. Witherspoon.
Deposited by the Naval Historical Foundation, 1949.

Marston, John,   1796–1885
Papers, 1850–62. 250 items.
Naval officer. Official correspondence, orders to duty, circulars, and general orders, relating to Marston's duties as senior officer of the North Atlantic Blockading Squadron, including plans for blockading Confederate ports. Correspondents include James F. Armstrong, Samuel L. Breese, Louis M. Goldsborough, Samuel V. Merrick, Garrett J. Pendergast, Silas H. Stringham, Isaac Toucey, and Gideon Welles.
Deposited by the Naval Historical Foundation, 1949.

Matthewson, Arthur,   1837–1920
Papers, 1861–65. 9 items.
Naval surgeon. Official correspondence concerning his assignments and examinations for promotions.
Deposited by the Naval Historical Foundation, 1949.

Mayrant, John,   1762–1836
Collection, 1926–27. 4 items.
Naval officer. Includes typescript copies of Mayrant's pension claim and biographical material extracted from the South Carolina Historical and Genealogical Magazine, April 1926, describing his services under John Paul Jones during the Revolutionary War.
Deposited by the Naval Historical Foundation, 1949.

McCleery, Robert W.,   d. 1863
Papers, ca. 1859–63. 3 items.
Naval officer. Letters received from Peter B. Robinson, U.S.S. Stettin, and George D. Emmons, U.S.S. Catskill, and an invitation to a dance for officers

serving on the U.S.S. Water Witch.
Deposited by the Naval Historical Foundation, 1964.

McCully, Newton Alexander, 1867–1951

Papers, 1917–27. 4 items.
Naval officer. Two personal diaries kept by McCully as commander, U.S. Naval Forces in Russia, and as representative to the peace commission in Paris (1918–20); printed matter relating to Russia; and a notebook kept by McCully as chief, U.S. Naval Mission, Brazil (1925–27).
Deposited by the Naval Historical Foundation, 1964.

McGowan, Samuel, 1870–1934

Papers, 1883–1943. 2000 items.
Naval officer. General correspondence, orders to duty, subject file, newspaper clippings, and miscellaneous material, chiefly 1900–20, relating to McGowan's duties as Paymaster General, U.S. Navy (1914–20), and to his interest in changing naval regulations he regarded as discriminatory. Correspondents include Philip Andrews, Bernard M. Baruch, Charles J. Bonaparte, Thomas J. Cowie, Josephus Daniels, Franklin D. Roosevelt, Benjamin R. Tillman, and Woodrow Wilson.
Finding aid in the Library.
Deposited by the Naval Historical Foundation, 1968.

McGregor, Charles, d. 1891

Correspondence, 1868–87. 2 items.
Naval officer. Holograph letter (Oct. 16, 1868) to McGregor from Ira Harris, U.S.S. Franklin, Mediterranean Fleet, and a copy of a letter (Mar. 4, 1887) of McGregor, U.S.S. Alliance, Anjouan, Comoro Islands, to the Sultan of Anjouan.
Deposited by the Naval Historical Foundation, 1964.

McNair, Frederick Vallette, 1882–1962

Papers, 1916–22. 700 items.
Naval officer. Naval signals regarding the sighting of enemy submarines or floating mines and their positions and printed matter concerning submarines, torpedoes, mines, and zeppelins, chiefly related to McNair's service on the U.S.S. Winslow in World War I.
Deposited by the Naval Historical Foundation, 1969.

McVay, Charles Butler, 1868–1949

Papers, 1896–1950. 900 items.
Naval officer. Official and general correspondence relating to McVay's duties as commander in chief of the Asiatic Fleet, 1929–30, newspaper

clippings, photos, and printed mater. The bulk of the papers is dated 1927–30. Correspondents include Charles Francis Adams, William Richards Castle, Edwin Sheddan Cunningham, Dwight Filley Davis, Lynn Winterdale Franklin, Nelson Trusler Johnson, and Howard Charles Kelly.

Finding aid in the Library.

Deposited by the Naval Historical Foundation, 1964.

Meigs, John Forsyth, 1848–1924

Papers, 1914–40. 1500 items.

Naval officer. Three letters, carbon and holograph drafts, and research notes for Meigs' book The Story of the Seaman (1924), together with research notes of Meigs' cousin, William L. Rodgers, who wrote the preface to the book.

Finding aid in the Library.

Deposited by the Naval Historical Foundation, 1953.

Melville, George Wallace, 1841–1912

Papers, 1871–1911. 125 items.

In part, transcripts.

Naval officer and explorer. Correspondence (ca. 45 items) and MSS. and TSS. of speeches and articles relating to the U.S. Navy and the construction of naval vessels. Correspondents include William E. Chandler, Ethan Allan Hitchcock, J. Sterling Morton, and Adlai E. Stevenson (1835–1914).

Deposited by the Naval Historical Foundation, 1972.

Merrill, Aaron Stanton, 1890–1961

Papers, 1925–63. 600 items.

Naval officer. General correspondence, orders to duty, speech file, citations, newspaper clippings, and printed matter, relating, in part, to Merrill's command of Task Force 39 and his role in the Battle of Empress Augusta Bay, Solomon Islands, during World War II. Correspondents include Elizabeth H. Cotten, Ernest M. Eller, John B. Heffernan, Dudley W. Knox, Samuel E. Morison, James W. Patton, and Elmer B. Potter.

Deposited by the Naval Historical Foundation, 1968.

Messersmith, John S.

Collection, 1837–54. 3 items.

Naval surgeon. Three commissions: one (1837) signed by Andrew Jackson, appointing Messersmith assistant surgeon, U.S. Navy; and two (1853, 1854) signed by Franklin Pierce, appointing Messersmith surgeon, U.S. Navy.

Deposited by the Naval Historical Foundation, 1964.

Miller, Cyrus Robinson,   1874–1923
   Collection, 1918. 2 items.
   Naval officer. Anecdote and a typewritten diary kept by Miller, commander of the U.S.S. Cleveland, while on convoy duty in the Atlantic. The diary contains messages from the bridge and from radio concerning speed, course, lights, and submarines.
   Deposited by the Naval Historical Foundation, 1964.

Moale, Edward,   d. 1903
   Journal, 1887–89. 1 v. (231 p.)
   Naval officer. Journal kept by Moale as a naval cadet on board the U.S.S. Vandalia, the U.S.S. Charleston, and the U.S.S. Mohican, containing abstracts, descriptions, and photos of the Hawaiian Islands, and descriptions of the U.S. Navy Yard, Mare Island, Calif.
   Deposited by the Naval Historical Foundation, 1964.

Morgan, James Morris
   Literary manuscript, undated. 1 item (8 p.)
   Transcript (typewritten)
   Confederate naval officer. Unsigned typescript attributed to Morgan concerning Clarence Cary's tours of duty on Confederate ships, particularly the C.S.S. Chickamauga. Constitutes p.17–24 of an unidentified larger work.
   Deposited by the Naval Historical Foundation, 1964.

Morse, John O.
   Papers, 1829–35. 142 items.
   Whaler captain. Financial papers of the whaling ship Hector, of New Bedford, Mass., commanded by Morse. Includes accounts, shipping papers, lists of the crew, and receipts for supplies and repairs.
   Deposited by the Naval Historical Foundation, 1964.

Mustin, Henry Croskey,   1874–1923
   Papers, 1886–1924. 2400 items.
   Naval officer and inventor. Correspondence, journals, lectures, articles, and other papers, chiefly 1903–20, relating to Mustin's inventions, especially his work in sighting equipment for naval ordnance, and his interest in aviation. Correspondents include Mustin's wife, Corinne, William S. Benson, Josephus Daniels, George N. Saegmuller, William S. Sims, William H. Stayton, John C. Watson, and Ernest Wilkinson.
   Register published by the Library in 1973.
   Deposited by the Naval Historical Foundation, 1962.

Nelson, Horatio,   1758–1805
Letter, 1801. 1 item.
Photocopy.
British naval officer. Letter to an unknown correspondent written by Nelson, H.M.S. Medusa, Aug. 21, 1801, concerning the range of his ship's guns.
Deposited by the Naval Historical Foundation, 1964.

Nepean, Evan,   1751–1822
Collection, 1803. 2 items.
Photocopies.
Clerk, British Admiralty. Letter and report from Nepean to Charles Cornwallis concering Robert Fulton, an American residing in Paris under the protection of the consul of the French Republic.
Deposited by the Naval Historical Foundation, 1961.

Nicholson, Reginald Fairfax,   1852–1939
Papers, 1873–1939. 20 items.
Naval officer. Correspondence, orders to duty, photographs, excerpt from Lowell Thomas' broadcast on Nicholson, and miscellany. Correspondence includes two letters from William H. Taft, one appointing Nicholson as commander in chief of the Asiatic Squadron and the second acknowledging receipt of Nicholson's resignation as Chief of the Bureau of Navigation; other correspondents include Josephus Daniels, Chester Nimitz, Franklin D. Roosevelt, and Theodore Roosevelt.
Deposited by the Naval Historical Foundation, 1964.

Nicholson, Sommerville,   1822–1905
Papers, 1839–81. 70 items.
Naval officer. Official, general, and family correspondence, and orders to duty. Correspondents include Nicholson's mother, Helen Lispinard Nicholson, Edward C. Anderson, John P. Kennedy, John Y. Mason, Matthew C. Perry, William Ballard Preston, Alexander C. Rhind, George M. Robeson, Christopher Raymond Perry Rodgers, Frank B. Rose, Isaac Toucey, Abel P. Upshur, Lewis Warrington, and Gideon Welles.
Deposited by the Naval Historical Foundation, 1964.

Nields, Henry C.,   d. 1880
Letter, 1867. 1 item.
Photocopy.
Naval officer. Letter (May 31, 1867) of Nields, U.S.S. Pawnee, South Atlantic Squadron, to his brother George, advising him to apply to the

U.S. Naval Academy.
Deposited by the Naval Historical Foundation, 1964.

Nonsuch (Schooner)

Logbook, 1812. 1 v. (103 p.)
Photocopy.
Logbook of the privateer Nonsuch, commanded by Henry Levely, describing encounters with British ships in the West Indies.
Deposited by the Naval Historical Foundation, 1964.

O'Neil, Charles, 1842–1927

Papers, 1833–1927. 5500 items.
Naval officer. Correspondence, diaries (1872–1927), subject files, photos, scrapbooks, financial records, and genealogical data. The papers relate chiefly to O'Neil's service as chief of the Navy's Bureau of Ordnance. Correspondents include George Dewey, Eugene Hale, John Davis Long, William Henry Moody, Franklin Delano Roosevelt, and Theodore Roosevelt.
Register published by the Library in 1967.
Deposited by the Naval Historical Foundation, 1954 and 1969.

Onis, Luis de, 1762–1827

Letter, 1812. 1 item.
Spanish minister to the U.S. Letter of Luis de Onis, Philadelphia, to British Vice Admiral Herbert Sawyer, Halifax, requesting that British ships not molest American vessels loaded with provisions bound for Portuguese and Spanish ports, with a copy of Sawyer's answer indicating compliance with Onis' request.
Deposited by the Naval Historical Foundation, 1964.

Parsons, William Sterling, 1901–1953

Papers, 1943–53. 1500 items.
Naval officer. Correspondence, supplemented by articles, clippings, a journal of Parson's activities (1951–52) as commander of Cruiser Division Six, U.S. Atlantic Fleet, and other material, relating, in part, to Parson's role in the development and testing of the atomic bomb (Manhattan Project, the bombing of Hiroshima, and Operation Crossroads). Correspondents include Bernard M. Baruch, Vannevar Bush, Robert B. Carney, Karl Compton, Ralph Earle, Jr., George Fielding Eliot, James Forrestal, James Gavin, Leslie R. Groves, David E. Lilienthal, Ernest K. Lindley, and Lewis L. Strauss.
Deposited by the Naval Historical Foundation, 1972.

Patterson, Daniel Todd, 1786–1839

Papers, 1802–1904. 1750 items.

Naval officer. Correspondence, journals, notebooks, reports, and printed matter, chiefly 1825–35, relating to Patterson's duties as fleet captain of the flagship U.S. Frigate Constitution and as commander of the Mediterranean Squadron. Correspondents include William W. Bleecker, Landon N. Carter, William M. Crane, Charles H. Jackson, John H. Jarvis, Edward Livingston, George Minor, Charles Morris, Joseph J. Nicholson, John B. Nicolson, Hiram Paulding, Matthew C. Perry, Richard S. Pinckney, David Porter, George C. Read, John Rodgers, Samuel L. Southard, and Richard Thomas.

Register published by the Library in 1970.

Deposited by the Naval Historical Foundation, 1951–52.

Paullin, Charles Oscar, 1868 or 9–1944
Papers, 1931 and undated. 4 items.

Author and historian. Typescripts of Paullin's unpublished books with corrections: "Colonial Army and Navy," "Military Forces of the American Revolution," and "Naval Establishments," together with a reprint of his article, Admiral Pierre Landis, published in the Catholic Historical Review, Oct. 1931.

Deposited by the Naval Historical Foundation, 1949.

Pelham, William
General order, 1864. 1 item.

Landsman. General order (Dec. 31, 1864) awarding the Medal of Honor to a number of servicemen, including Pelham, who had distinguished himself as a landsman on board the U.S. steam sloop Hartford in engagements in Mobile Bay, Aug. 5, 1864.

Deposited by the Naval Historical Foundation, 1961.

Péralte, Charlemagne Masséna, d. 1919
Letter, 1919. 1 item.
Photocopy.

Commander in chief, Haitian guerrillas. Letter of Péralte to Gen. Démosthènes Médinard naming Médinard Chief of the Third Division operating against the American forces.

Deposited by the Naval Historical Foundation, 1964.

Perkins, George Hamilton, 1835–1899
The Isabel Perkins Anderson collection of the papers of George Hamilton Perkins, 1857–1936. 500 items.

Naval officer. Correspondence, printed matter, clippings, photos, and miscellaneous material. Includes letters from Perkins to his wife, Anna, and daughter, Isabel Perkins Anderson, and letters from Isabel Perkins

Anderson to Daniel Chester French, concerning commissions for statues of her father, and to Carroll Storrs Alden, Perkins' biographer. Other correspondents in the collection include Willard H. Brownson, George Dewey, Stephen B. Luce, Victor H. Metcalf, John H. Upshur, and Beekman Winthrop.
Deposited by the Naval Historical Foundation, 1964.

Perry, Matthew Calbraith, 1794–1858
Papers, 1839–1931. 10 items.
In part, transcripts.
Naval officer and commander in chief of negotiations with the Japanese for the treaty signed in 1854. Official correspondence; an order book kept on board the U.S.F. Cumberland at Vera Cruz (1847–48); and printed matter from the American-Japan Society. Represented in the correspondence are Perry Belmont, Gouverneur Kemble, Eugene A. Vail, and Ken Kichi Yoshizawa.
Deposited by the Naval Historical Foundation, 1964.

Perry, Oliver Hazard, 1785–1819
Collection, 1845. 4 items.
Naval officer. Two documents concerning a mortgage signed by Perry's widow, Elizabeth Champlin Mason Perry, and two photos of a jug with Perry's likeness on it.
Deposited by the Naval Historical Foundation, 1949.

Pettengill, George Tilford, 1877–1959
Collection, 1863–1937. 7 items.
In part, photocopies.
Naval officer. Letters concerning sanitation and equipment, photos, and an article about Thomas Tingey.
Deposited by the Naval Historical Foundation, 1964.

Phillips, Richard Helsden, 1906–
Papers, 1917–58. 600 items.
Naval officer. Subject file relating to Phillips' command of the U.S.S. Belleau Wood and the U.S.S. Shaw during World War II, speech and article file, and printed matter.
Deposited by the Naval Historical Foundation, 1968.

Phoenix, Lloyd, d. 1926
Collection, 1921–27. 2 items.
Naval officer. Letter of Phoenix to James M. Morgan, concerning ships, and a biographical sketch of Phoenix' life by Morgan, relating Phoenix'

experiences in the Civil War, his resignation from the Navy in 1865, and his 50 years of sailing his own yachts.

Deposited by the Naval Historical Foundation, 1964.

Pinkney, Ninian, 1811–1877
Papers, 1830–78. 900 items.

Naval surgeon. Correspondence, speeches, articles, and notes, chiefly 1840–70, relating to Pinkney's surgical cases in Peru, his observations on the Mexican and Civil Wars, his plan to reorganize the U.S. Medical Corps, and his interest in politics. Includes family correspondence. Correspondents include George Bancroft, Henry Clay, Samuel Hambleton, Matthew C. Perry, and Gideon Welles.

Finding aid in the Library.

Deposited by the Naval Historical Foundation, 1949, 1957.

Pollock, Edwin Taylor, 1870–1943
Papers, 1898–1939. 18 items.

In part, transcripts (typewritten)

Naval officer. Extracts from Pollock's letters concerning the Spanish-American War in the Caribbean, two letters about the U.S.S. Mariveles and the Santo Niño, and letters exchanged with Edward W. Hanson.

Deposited by the Naval Historical Foundation, 1964.

Pook family
Collection, 1937. 5 items.

Biographical material on Samuel Moore Pook (1804–1878) and his son, Samuel Hartt Pook (1827–1901), naval constructors. Samuel M. Pook designed clipper ships and served with John Rodgers in Cairo, Ill. (1861); Samuel H. Pook designed the U.S.S. Galena and supervised the building of ironclad vessels.

Deposited by the Naval Historical Foundation, 1949.

Porter family
Papers, 1811–81. 600 items.

Papers, chiefly 1867–81, of David Porter (1780–1843) and his son, David Dixon Porter (1813–1891), naval officers and authors. David Porter's papers consist of letters written to his wife, Evelina, and to Samuel Hambleton, James P. McCorkle, and George W. Walker, a draft of his resignation as commander in chief of the Mexican Navy, and his will. David Dixon Porter's papers include letterbooks, a letter to his wife George Ann, a draft of a letter to William H. Seward, and printed general orders.

Finding aid in the Library.

Deposited by the Naval Historical Foundation, 1949.

Powel, Mary Edith,   1846–1931
    Collection, 1747–1922. 32,000 items.
    Collector of naval history. Correspondence, biographical data on American and foreign naval officers, newspaper and magazine clippings, illustrations, photos, commissions, autographs, pamphlets, and notes, chiefly 1890–99. Newspaper clippings form the largest part of the collection. Subjects include U.S. and foreign naval officers, ships, disasters at sea, Arctic explorations in the 1890's, Navy educational institutions, marine natural history, and the merchant marine. Correspondents include Walter R. Benjamin, M. Bruckner, and Stephen B. Luce.
    Register published by the Library in 1971.
    Deposited by the Naval Historical Foundation, 1963.

Pratt, William Veazie,   1869–1957
    Papers, 1862–1963. 200 items.
    Naval officer. Chiefly articles by Pratt relating to seapower, disarmament, and American's role in keeping the peace, written during his service as President of the Naval War College (1925–27), commander in chief of the Battle Fleet and U.S. Fleet (1928–30), and chief of naval operations (1930–33). Includes autobiographical and genealogical material, speeches and lectures by Pratt and others, naval orders, printed matter, and some papers of Pratt's father, Nichols Pratt, relating to his naval service during and after the Civil War.
    Deposited by the Naval Historical Foundation, 1969.

Radford, William,   1809–1890
    Papers, 1847–90. 53 items.
    Naval officer. Correspondence, orders to duty, and other material, chiefly relating to Radford's naval career and the Civil War. Correspondents include Solomon D. Belton, Walter D. C. Boggs, Andrew H. Foote, Gustavus Fox, William W. Low, Hiram Paulding, George M. Robeson, Cornelius K. Stirling, William G. Temple, and Gideon Welles.
    Deposited by the Naval Historical Foundation, 1949.

Rae, Charles Whitesides,   d. 1908
    Journal, 1870–71. 1 v. (ca. 50 p.)
    Naval officer. Journal kept by Rae of the survey of the Isthmus of Tehuantepec, Mexico. Includes personal observations of the houses, the weather, and the Indians of Tehuantepec.
    Deposited by the Naval Historical Foundation, 1949.

Rawson, Edward Kirk,   1846–1934
    Article, undated. 1 item.

Naval chaplain and professor at the U.S. Naval Academy. Typescript, with emendations and covering note, of an article by Rawson concerning the Penobscot Bay Expedition of 1779, commanded by Dudley Saltonstall.
Deposited by the Naval Historical Foundation, 1950.

Reid, William L.
Letters, 1852. 14 items.
Photocopies.
Family letters of William L. Reid to his brothers, Samuel and Bertrand Reid, sons of Samuel Chester Reid (1783–1861), sea captain and sailing master of the U.S. Navy, concerning family matters and current political affairs.
Deposited by the Naval Historical Foundation, 1964.

Remey, George Collier,   1841–1928
Collection, 1902–35. 1 item.
Naval officer. Typescript of Remey's "Reminiscences," an account of his Civil War experiences, bound with two letters (1935) of Reginald R. Belknap.
Deposited by the Naval Historical Foundation, 1964.

Reynolds, William,   1815–1879
Collection, 1877–80. 2 items.
Naval officer. May 1887 issue of the Japan Punch and a reprint (1880) of William Reynolds, Rear-Admiral U.S.N., by J. G. Rosengarten.
Deposited by the Naval Historical Foundation, 1964.

Richardson, Holden Chester,   1878–1960
Papers, 1844–1946. 3600 items.
Naval officer. General and family correspondence, speeches, articles, and books, subject file, and miscellaneous material, chiefly 1897–1944, relating primarily to Richardson's activities in aeronautics. Correspondents include James E. Fetchet, Ernest J. King, Ernest M. Pace, Edward T. Pachasa, Carl J. Wenzinger, and Isaac I. Yates.
Finding aid in the Library.
Deposited by the Naval Historical Foundation, 1967.

Ridgely, Charles Goodwin,   1784–1848
Papers, 1815–26. 4 items.
Naval officer. Letterbook, personal journal, and two letters, chiefly relating to Ridgely's command of the U.S.F. Constellation, South American Squadron, 1820–22, and recording his observations on the Navy's Latin American policy.

Register published by the Library in 1970.
Deposited by the Naval Historical Foundation, 1949.

Ridgely, Frank Eugene,   1875–1926
Papers, 1898–1924. 150 items.
Naval officer. Orders to duty, newspaper clippings, and a World War I
map of Europe.
Finding aid in the Library.
Deposited by the Naval Historical Foundation, 1949.

Riggs, Arthur Stanley,   1879–1952
Papers, 1929–52. 900 items.
In part, photocopies.
Naval reserve officer and author. Chiefly material concerning Riggs
unpublished book, "Drake of the Seven Seas." Includes notes, drafts and
MS. of the book, correspondence, articles, clippings, receipts, printed mat-
ter, maps, and photos, chiefly 1949–51. Correspondents include Ricardo J.
Alfaro, Herbert E. Bolton, George T. Bye, Helen Cam, Jacob Canter,
John A. Hamilton, Leonard B. Loeb, John Frank Stevens, Earl O. Titus,
and Arthur E. Young.
Finding aid in the Library.
Deposited by the Naval Historical Foundation, 1955.

Riley, William Edward,   1897–
Papers, 1941–48. 800 items.
Marine officer. Correspondence, operation plans and reports, memoranda,
notes, maps, photos, and other material, relating to Riley's command of
the South Pacific Forces, the operations of the Third Fleet, and the invasions
of the Philippine and Ulithi Islands during World War II. Includes copies
of speeches by James Forrestal, William F. Halsey, Thomas C. Kinkaid,
William D. Leahy, and Kenneth C. Royall.
Deposited by the Naval Historical Foundation, 1968.

Rodgers family
Papers, 1788–1944. 15,500 items.
Correspondence, notebooks, biographical material, speeches, articles, radio
broadcasts, book reviews, journals, notes and drafts relating to the published
works of William Ledyard Rodgers, and other papers, of John Rodgers
(1773–1838), John Rodgers (1812–1882), William Ledyard Rodgers
(1860–1944), John Augustus Rodgers (1848–1933), and John Rodgers
(1881–1926), relating to their naval careers. Includes some correspondence
of the Hodge family, Matthew C. and Oliver H. Perry, and other Rodgers
relatives. Correspondents include Louis Agassiz, Daniel Ammen, William

Bainbridge, William S. Benson, John M. Brooke, James Buchanan, Josephus Daniels, Charles H. Davis, Stephen Decatur, Mrs. Samuel F. Du Pont, David G. Farragut, Harry A. Garfield, William Henry Harrison, Charles E. Hughes, Dudley W. Knox, Alexander Slidell Mackenzie, John T. McLaughlin, John Bassett Moore, Winfield Scott, William S. Sims, Samuel L. Southard, Charles Sumner, Gideon Welles, and George G. Wilson.

Register published by the Library in 1972.

Deposited by the Naval Historical Foundation, 1950, with additions, 1964, 1967, and 1969.

Rodgers, William Tennent
Papers, 1813–17. 6 items.

Naval officer. U.S.S. Peacock logbook (1814), drawings, newspaper clippings, and private journal kept by Rodgers aboard the U.S.S. Peacock (1813–15), brig Wilson (1816), and U.S.S. Boxer (1817). The journal describes battles in the War of 1812 and prizes captured by the U.S.S. Peacock.

Deposited by the Naval Historical Foundation, 1956.

Roe, Francis Asbury,   1823–1901
Papers, 1842–1901. 500 items.

Naval officer. Correspondence, journals, notebooks, and other papers, chiefly 1846–69. Includes descriptions of Roe's cruises and an account of an engagement between the U.S.S. Sassacus and the C.S.S. Albemarle in 1864.

Register published by the Library in 1970.

Deposited by the Naval Historical Foundation, 1949–69.

Rowan, Stephen Clegg,   1808–1890
Papers, 1826–90. 4 items.

Naval officer. Private journals kept on board the U.S.S. Vincennes (1826–28), U.S.S. Delaware (1841–43), U.S.S. Cyane (1845), and U.S.S. Piscataque (1868), describing Rowan's cruises and activities; and a letterbook (1852–90) containing orders to duty, notes on his 64 years of naval service, and copies of letters to Ambrose E. Burnside, Salmon P. Chase, James C. Dobbin, John A. Dahlgren, Gustavus V. Fox, Louis M. Goldsborough, David D. Porter, Robert W. Shufeldt, Isaac Toucey, Gideon Welles, and William C. Whitney.

Finding aid in the Library.

Deposited by the Naval Historical Foundation, 1969.

Russell, John Henry,   1827–1897
Papers, 1861–75. 18 items.

Naval officer. Official correspondence, orders to duty, general orders, and diagram of the batteries of Vicksburg, Miss. (1861–64). Correspondents include Henry H. Bell, John A. Dahlgren, David G. Farragut, Cadwalader Ringgold, George M. Robeson, Gideon Welles, and John A. Winslow.

Deposited by the Naval Historical Foundation, 1949.

Ryan, George Parker,   1842–1877

Papers, 1860–1952. 75 items.

Naval officer. Family and general correspondence, journal, photos, newspaper clippings, and printed matter, relating, in part, to naval observations of the eclipse of Venus at Kerguelen (1874) and to the wreck of the U.S.S. Huron, in which Ryan was lost. Includes a few papers of his son, George Whitehouse Ryan.

Deposited by the Naval Historical Foundation, 1970.

Sargent, Nathan,   1849–1907

Papers, 1866–1957. 2700 items.

Naval officer. Correspondence, diaries, journals, MS. of an unpublished book, "Donihle or an American Baronet," photos, memorabilia, scrapbooks, and printed matter, relating to Sargent's naval duties and his tours aboard the U.S.S. Alaska (1873) and the U.S.S. Lancaster (1884). The bulk of the papers is dated 1880–1905. Correspondents include John Burns, Mortimer E. Cooley, George Dewey, Mildred Dewey, William H. Emory, David J. Hill, Cyrus E. Lothrop, Sidney A. Staunton, and John G. Walker.

Finding aid in the Library.

Deposited by the Naval Historical Foundation, 1950–64.

Sawyer, Horace Bucklin,   1797–1860

Papers, 1812–1950. 900 items.

Naval officer. Correspondence and diaries ("Memorandum Books"), chiefly 1814–56. Includes letterbooks (1813–57, 1842–59, 1855–59) containing copies of incoming and outgoing letters, both official and personal, newspaper clippings, and sketches documenting Sawyer's experiences in the War of 1812; and diaries (1842–58) recording Sawyer's observations on the Mexican War, political events in the U.S., revolutions in Europe, earthquakes in the West Indies, John Charles Frémont's court-martial, and other contemporary events. Includes some papers relating to other family members: notes of naval records and photos of George Augustus Sawyer (d. 1904), paymaster in the U.S. Navy; obituary of architect Philip Sawyer (d. 1949); and genealogical material. Correspondents include William Bainbridge, Henry E. Ballard, George Bancroft, Abijah Bigelow, Benjamin Crowninshield, Jefferson Davis, James C. Dobbin, Lawrence Kearny, Edmund P. Kennedy, John Y. Mason, Samuel S. Phelps, Joel R. Poinsett, Charles G. Ridgely, Winfield Scott, William S. Shaw, Samuel L. Southard, Charles Stewart, Isaac Toucey, Abel P. Upshur, and Gideon Welles.

Finding aid in the Library.
Deposited by the Naval Historical Foundation, 1955–61.

Schoonmaker, Cornelius Marius,   1839–1889
Papers, 1833–1931. 1400 items.

Naval officer. Official and other correspondence, scrapbooks, and MS. of Schoonmaker's biography, written by his father, Marius Schoonmaker. Correspondents include William E. Chandler, John A. Dahlgren, Thomas A. Dornin, David G. Farragut, Louis M. Goldsborough, John C. Howell, Richard Thompson, Isaac Toucey, Gideon Welles, and William C. Whitney.
Finding aid in the Library.
Deposited by the Naval Historical Foundation, 1950.

Selfridge, Thomas Oliver,   1804–1902
Papers, 1809–1927. 750 items.

Naval officer. Correspondence, journals, logbooks, and notebooks, chiefly 1809–70, relating to Selfridge's naval career. Includes material relating to the U.S.S. Mississippi and the Mare Island Navy Yard, which were commanded by Selfridge, and to the Naval Examining Board over which he presided. Correspondents include Henry E. Ballard, George E. Belknap, A. F. Crossman, F. S. Grier, David Dixon Porter, and Thomas Oliver Selfridge, Jr. (1836–1924).
Register published by the Library.
Deposited by the Naval Historical Foundation, 1949.

Selfridge, Thomas Oliver,   1836–1924
Papers, 1852–1927. 1900 items.

Naval officer and explorer. Correspondence, journals, logbooks, notebooks, scrapbooks, and miscellaneous papers, concentrated in the period 1858–80, relating to the Darien expedition (1869–74) headed by Selfridge and given the task of surveying the Isthmus of Darien (Panama) as a site for an interoceanic canal. Includes material relating to the sinking of the U.S.F. Cumberland by the C.S.S. Merrimack in 1862, the purchase of the John T. Pickett papers by the United States, and Selfridge's court-martial in 1888. Correspondents include Daniel Ammen, Judah P. Benjamin, Edward Knight Collins, George Davidson, Walter E. Evans, Gustavus Vasa Fox, James Bicheno Francis, John Bloomfield Jervis, Benjamin Henry Latrobe, Benjamin Osgood Peirce, John Luke Porter, Thomas Oliver Selfridge, Sr. (1804–1902), and J. Dutton Steele.
Register published by the Library in 1969.
Deposited by the Naval Historical Foundation, 1949.

Sellers, David Foote,   1874–1949
Papers, 1860–1949. 6500 items.

Naval officer. Correspondence, journals, photos, scrapbooks, and newspaper clippings, concentrated in the period 1927–38, and relating to Sellers' naval career. Includes papers relating to his service in the Spanish-American War, his assignments as naval aide to the White House in 1907 and aide to the commander of the German fleet visiting the United States in 1912, his World War I service, his commands of the Special Service Squadron and the U.S. Fleet, and his service as superintendent of the U.S. Naval Academy. About half the correspondence relates to his duty with the Special Service Squadron during the Nicaraguan internal troubles (1927–29). Correspondents include Charles F. Adams, H. A. Baldridge, Hanson Baldwin, Richard E. Byrd, Jr., H. W. Dodds, and Dudley W. Knox.

Register published by the Library in 1969.

Deposited by the Naval Historical Foundation, 1951, 1963.

Semmes, Alexander A., d. 1885

Order books, 1869–71. 2 items.

Naval officer. Order books of the U.S.S. Portsmouth, commanded by Semmes, containing copies of orders, specifications, courts-martial, and some correspondence.

Deposited by the Naval Historical Foundation, 1964.

Shafroth, John Franklin, 1887–1967

Papers, 1926–45. 1800 items.

Naval officer. Official correspondence, memoranda, directives, and reports sent to William F. Halsey and Chester W. Nimitz, relating primarily to Shafroth's experiences as a commander in the South Pacific and head of a task group which conducted the first heavy bombardment of Japan during World War II. Includes 11 vols. relating to Shafroth's course work at the Army War College (1926–28).

Register published by the Library in 1973.

Deposited by the Naval Historical Foundation, 1968.

Shaw, John, 1773–1823

Papers, 1798–1895. 1200 items.

Naval officer. Correspondence (official and private), journal, notebooks, reports, biographical data, and miscellany, relating primarily to Shaw's command of the New Orleans station (1810–13) and the Boston Navy Yard (1819–22). The bulk of the papers is dated 1810-22. Correspondents include Samuel Angus, William Bainbridge, James Biddle, Amos Binney, Isaac Chauncey, Henry Denison, Jesse D. Elliott, Thomas Fillebrown, Charles W. Goldsborough, Moses Green, Samuel Hambleton, Isaac Hull, Thomas Macdonough, Alexander Murray, David Porter, James Renshaw, John Rodgers, Joseph B. Shaw, Benjamin Thomas, Smith Thompson, and George A. Wise.

Finding aid in the Library.
Deposited by the Naval Historical Foundation, 1949–50.

Sherman, William Tecumseh,   1820–1891

Letter, 1887. 1 item.

Army officer. Letter (Jan. 11, 1887) of Sherman to Ammen Farenholt, Walden, Mass., concerning qualifications of voters.

Deposited by the Naval Historical Foundation, 1964.

Shufeldt, Robert Wilson,   1822–1895

Papers, 1836–1910. 15,000 items.

Naval officer, explorer, and diplomat. Correspondence (official, personal, and family), journals, diaries, notebooks, logbooks, subject files, newspaper clippings, and printed matter. Includes material concerning Mason A. Shufeldt and his explorations in Africa, and some papers of Mary (Miller) Shufeldt. The official correspondence is composed primarily of quasi-official communications and orders to duty. Topics represented include the 19th century Navy, its growth and development; Civil War naval and diplomatic activities; foreign relations in the 1870's and 1880's, especially with Africa and Asia; and the Tehuantepec Mexico Survey Expedition, 1870–71. Also documented are Shufeldt's assignment as consul general to Cuba, 1861–63, his mission to Mexico, 1862, and the world cruise of the U.S.S. Ticonderoga, 1878–80. Correspondents include Edward Atkinson, Alexander Dallas Bache, George Bancroft, Henry Haywood Bell, William Bradford, Cyrus Clay Carpenter, Li Hung Chang, John Adolphus Dahlgren, David Glasgow Farragut, Hamilton Fish, Peter A. Hargous, David Henshaw, Alfred Hopkins, Thornton Alexander Jenkins, William Slidell Mackenzie, M. Konde Masuki, William Henry Seward, Truman Smith, B. F. Stevens, John Grimes Walker, Gideon Welles, and John N. Wolf.

Register published by the Library in 1969.

Deposited by the Naval Historical Foundation, 1949, 1952, and 1954.

Sicard, Montgomery,   1836–1900

Papers, 1800–1948. 1200 items.

Naval officer. Official and general correspondence, subject file, and miscellaneous material, chiefly 1870–98. Includes Sicard's diagrams and memorandums for breech-loading howitzers and his plans for steel armorplate for ships. In his plans for steel plates are notes, memorandums, letters, blueprints, and a corrected galley for "Specifications for Armour for the United States Navy." Financial papers include letters from Sicard's brothers, Stephen and George J. Sicard, and his brother-in-law, William Floyd; tax receipts; receipts for household goods; and papers on profits, investments, and property. The miscellaneous material includes trade papers of Sicard's father, Stephen Sicard, and material relating to management of the Floyd's property in New York. The general correspondence includes several letters exchanged with family members, including Sicard's wife, Elizabeth (Floyd) Sicard, and their children, William Floyd, Montgomery, and Eleanor L. Sicard. Other correspondents include William E. Chandler, William Folger, William H. Hunt, Charles O'Neil, David D. Porter, and Asa Walker.

Finding aid in the Library.

Deposited by the Naval Historical Foundation, 1964.

Sims, William Sowden,   1858–1936

Papers, 1856–1951. 43,000 items.

Naval officer. Official and personal correspondence, MSS. of writings, reports, military orders, notes, clippings, invitations, and memorabilia, documenting Sims' naval career, including his activities as intelligence officer of the U.S.S. Charleston at the China Station (1895–96), naval attaché at Paris, Madrid, and St. Petersburg (1896–1900), and commander of U.S. naval forces in Europe during World War I (1917–19). The bulk of the material is dated from 1900 to 1935 and provides information on Sims' interest in naval reforms. Includes correspondence and social calendars of Sims' wife, Anne Hitchcock Sims. Correspondents include W. F. Arnold, John V. Babcock, Lewis Bayly, William S. Benson, Josephus Daniels, W. Atlee Edwards, Bradley A. Fiske, William F. Fullam, Herbert Hoover, Tracy B. Kittredge, Alfred T. Mahan, Ridley McLean, William V. Pratt, J. R. Poinsett Pringle, Henry Reuterdahl, Kenneth Roberts, Franklin D. Roosevelt, and Theodore Roosevelt.

Register published by the Library in 1971.

Deposited by the Naval Historical Foundation, 1961–72.

Smith, Daniel Angell,   1839–1901

Papers, 1863–1905. 38 items.

Naval officer. Family correspondence, orders to duty, and miscellaneous material. Includes letters to his sister concerning the blockade of Charleston, S.C. (1863–64) and an account of the Battle of Manila Bay (1898).

Deposited by the Naval Historical Foundation, 1964.

Smith, Stuart Farrar,   1874–1951

Papers, 1860–1951. 300 items.

Naval officer. Correspondence, diaries concerning the Naval Armistice Conference (1918-19), passports, commissions, photos, programs, invitations, and memorabilia. Includes leaves from a notebook containing data on ships of the Civil War period.

Deposited by the Naval Historical Foundation, 1964.

Snow, Elliot, 1866–1939
Papers, 1790–1942. 9450 items.
Naval officer and author. Correspondence, logbooks, speech, article, and book file, newspaper clippings, printed matter, and scrapbooks, chiefly 1920–30, relating to the history and restoration of the U.S. Frigate Constitution. Includes papers of Horatio D. Smith (1845–1918), officer in the U.S. Revenue Cutter Service, and a small group of papers of Josiah Fox (1763–1847), naval constructor. Snow's correspondents include William Alcott, Philip Andrews, George A. Bahn, James Barnes, Jouett T. Cannon, Henry T. Claus, William E. Foster, Letitia A. Humphreys, Constance Lathrop, Paul C. Nicholson, Haviland Hull Platt, Albert S. Snow, William F. Spicer, Karl Vogel, and Curtis D. Wilbur.
Register published by the Library in 1969.
Deposited by the Naval Historical Foundation, 1949–63.

Spence, Robert Traill, ca. 1785–1827
Letterbook, 1822–23. 1 item. (ca. 200 p.)
Photocopies.
Naval officer. Letterbook kept by Spence while serving as commander, U.S.S. Cyane, during a tour of the West Indies to protect American lives and interests, and during a tour of West Africa to prevent the transport of slaves and to protect the settlement in Liberia. Includes outgoing letters to Francisco González de Linares, Judah Lord, Courtland Parker, Carlos Sowblette, and Smith Thompson.
Deposited by the Naval Historical Foundation, 1964.

Sperry, Charles Stillman, 1847–1911
Papers, 1899. 2 items.
Naval officer. Holograph manuscript (24 p.) and typewritten copy concerning Sperry's command of the U.S.S. Yorktown during the Spanish-American War.
Deposited by the Naval Historical Foundation, 1949 and 1950.

Standley, William Harrison, 1872–1963
Papers, 1895–1963. 2500 items.
Naval officer and U.S. Ambassador to the U.S.S.R. Personal and general correspondence, drafts of Standley's books Admiral Ambassador to Russia (1955) and his autobiography Admiral Standley, Early Life and Naval Career, speeches, articles, naval orders, news releases, reports, printed matter, and other papers, chiefly 1940–60, dealing primarily with Standley's interest in U.S. naval power in the 1930's, his concern with U.S. foreign relations with Germany in 1940 and the U.S.S.R. after World War II, and his involvement in anti-Communist organizations in the 1950's. Correspondents include Reginald R. Belknap, Frank N. D. Buchman, John G. Crommelin, Loy H.

Henderson, Roy W. Howard, William E. Jenner, William Knowland, William Stanley, David I. Walsh, and Russell Wilson.

Register published by the Library in 1973.

Deposited by the Naval Historical Foundation, 1969–73.

Stellwagen, Daniel S.,   d. 1828

Collection, 1814–27. 4 items.

Photocopies.

Naval officer. Two letters, signal book, and orders of the third division of galleys, which Stellwagen served as commander in the battle of Lake Champlain (War of 1812). Correspondents include Joseph S. Cannon and Thomas Macdonough.

Deposited by the Naval Historical Foundation, 1964.

Stevens family

Papers, 1810–1952. 35 items.

In part, photocopies.

Correspondence and other papers of Thomas Holdup Stevens (1795–1841), Thomas Holdup Stevens II (1819–1896), and Thomas Holdup Stevens III (1848–1914), naval officers. Includes letters (1810–15) of Thomas Holdup Stevens to Benjamin Crowninshield and Ralph Izard; letter (1816) of Daniel Stevens, adoptive father of Thomas Holdup Stevens, to Ebenezer Sage; letters (1844–64) to Thomas Holdup Stevens II from John Y. Mason, C. R. Perry Rodgers, and Lucius Waterman; biographical material; affidavit of Thomas Holdup Stevens, who commanded the U.S.S. Trippe at the Battle of Lake Erie, 1813, concerning the conduct of Jesse D. Elliott in that battle; diagrams of the Battle of Lake Erie; pamphlet by Thomas Holdup Stevens II describing the wreck of the Marie Helena on Christmas Island, Jan. 4, 1848; typescript of "Hoisting the Flag in Honolulu" (July 1898) by Thomas Holdup Stevens III; photos; newspaper clippings (1875–1920); and a copy of the Great Seal of the Confederate States.

Deposited by the Naval Historical Foundation, 1950 and 1964.

Stillman, George,   ca. 1750–1804

Papers, 1775–1803. 54 items.

Photocopies of originals in the New York Public Library.

Officer in the Continental Massachusetts Militia and the Continental Marines. Correspondence, diary, commissions, and a poem. Subjects include the defense of Machias, Mass. (later, Maine), a battle near Charlestown, Mass., and Stillman's cruises. Correspondents include William Allen, John Hancock, and Paul Revere.

Deposited by the Naval Historical Foundation, 1954.

Strauss, Joseph, 1861–1948

Papers, 1881–1922. 25 items.

Naval officer. Correspondence from the period Strauss served as commander in chief, U.S. Asiatic Fleet, relating to the defense of the Philippine Islands and to civil strife in China (1922), three notebooks kept by Strauss as a midshipman, and two articles by Strauss.

Deposited by the Naval Historical Foundation, 1961.

Susquehanna (U.S.S.)

Collection, 1853–65. 3 items.

Photocopies and transcript.

Chinese letter (1853), with a typed translation, from the files of Franklin Buchanan, commander (1852–53) of the U.S.S. Susquehanna, and a photo (1865) of the officers of the U.S.S. Susquehanna.

Deposited by the Naval Historical Foundation, 1964.

Symington, Powers, 1872–1957

Papers, 1916–57. 38 items.

Naval officer. Correspondence, notes, and articles relating to military matters. Subjects of Symington's notes and articles include gunnery, submarines, mine lookouts, modern army morale, admirals, defense, and military training. Correspondents are Louis E. Denfeld, Ernest J. King, and Charles S. Thomas.

Deposited by the Naval Historical Foundation, 1960–61.

Tarbell, John F.

Journal, 1876–77. 1 v. (61 p.)

Naval officer. Personal journal kept by Tarbell on board the U.S.S. Gettysburg describing Gibraltar, Portugal, Spain, Italy, and France, and receptions, balls, and carnivals.

Deposited by the Naval Historical Foundation, 1964.

Taussig, Edward David, 1947–1921

Papers, 1867–1900. 33 items.

Naval officer. Family correspondence, log of the U.S.S. Wateree, and letter of commendation. Subjects include the earthquake in Arica, Chile (1868), and descriptions of battles with insurgents in the Philippine Islands (1900).

Deposited by the Naval Historical Foundation, 1964.

Taussig, Joseph Knefler, 1877–1947

Papers, 1921. 1 item.

Naval officer. Speech entitled "Operators of American Destroyers Based

on Queenstown," given before officers at staff college, San Diego, California, 1921.
Deposited by the Naval Historical Foundation, 1949.

Taylor, Henry Clay,   1845–1904
Papers, 1862–1904. 300 items.
In part, transcripts.
Naval officer. Correspondence, diary, writings by Taylor including a novel entitled Naroonya, photos, and printed matter relating to the Spanish-American War. The bulk of the papers is dated 1897–1900, when Taylor commanded the U.S.S. Indiana. Correspondents include George Dewey, Stephen B. Luce, Christopher Raymond Perry Rodgers, and William Thomas Sampson.
Finding aid in the Library.
Deposited by the Naval Historical Foundation, 1954.

Taylor, Montgomery Meigs,   1869–1952
Papers, 1890–1936. 1200 items.
Naval officer and commander in chief of the Asiatic Fleet. Official correspondence, personal letters (1931–33) reflecting life in the Orient, orders, financial papers, reports entitled Outline of Action which document Taylor's activities during the dispute (1932) between China and Japan over control of Shanghai, his Cadet journal, notebooks, articles, speeches, records relating to his tours of duty in the Philippines (1898), Scotland (1918), and the Panama Canal Zone (1922), scrapbooks, and photos. Names represented include Charles Francis Adams, Nelson Trusler Johnson, William Veazie Pratt, and William Harrison Standley.
Finding aid in the Library.
Deposited by the Naval Historical Foundation, 1953.

Terrett, Colville,   d. 1860
Papers, 1850–59. 6 items.
Naval officer. Letters of Terrett to his wife written during his tours of duty in Greece, Hong Kong, Boston, and Valparaiso, and a photo. Subjects include ports of call in the Mediterranean Sea, China and the Chinese, William B. Reed's negotiations with China, and a celebration of Chilean independence.
Deposited by the Naval Historical Foundation, 1964.

Thatcher, Henry Knox,   1806–1880
Agreement, Feb. 6, 1866. 1 item.
Naval officer. Agreement between Thatcher, commander of the Gulf

Squadron, and S. Colburn concerning the raising of two torpedo boats sunk in Mobile Bay.
Deposited by the Naval Historical Foundation, 1961.

Thomas, Charles Mitchell,   1846–1908
Papers, 1907–08. 80 items.
Naval officer. Thomas' letters to his wife, Ruth Simpson Thomas, giving descriptions of receptions and dinners, and details of Robley D. Evans' illness; copies of remarks made at receptions; newspaper clippings; and memorabilia, including invitations, calling cards, programs, menus, and postcards, relating to visits to Brazil, Peru, and Trinidad made by the 2d Squadron, U.S. Atlantic Fleet, which Thomas served as commander.
Deposited by the Naval Historical Foundation, 1968 and 1970.

Thomas, Gardner,   d. 1829
Papers, 1815–32. 11 items.
Naval officer. Correspondence, chiefly concerned with Thomas' financial estate following his death in 1829; Thomas' commission as purser signed by James Madison; memorandum; and three receipts. Correspondents include James M. Halsey, Sarah Hopkins, and Amos Kendall.
Deposited by the Naval Historical Foundation, 1949.

Tingey, Thomas,   1750–1829
Papers, 1795–1827. 55 items.
In part, photocopies.
Naval officer. Journal (1795–96) kept on board the U.S.S. Ganges of a voyage from Philadelphia to Madeira, Bengal, Madras, and return to Philadelphia; letters (1797–1827) of Tingey to his daughters, Hannah Tingey and Margaret Gay Wingate, and to his son-in-law, Joseph F. Wingate; and a letter (1801) of Tingey to Lt. John McRea, commander of the U.S.F. Congress, concerning regulations to be established on the ship.
Deposited by the Naval Historical Foundation, 1970.

Truxtun, Thomas,   1755–1822
Papers, 1796–1885. 13 items.
In part, transcripts.
Correspondence (1799–1817), property share (1796), funeral announcement, and printed matter concerning Truxtun (1806) and his grandson, William Talbot Truxtun (1885). Correspondents include George Balfour, David M. Clarkson, Joseph Cornman, Alexander Murray, William Patterson, Benjamin Stoddert, and Samuel Swartwout.
Deposited by the Naval Historical Foundation, 1952.

Turner, Thomas,   1808–1883

Thomas Turner—David R. Stewart collection, 1834–35. 27 items.

In part, transcripts.

Reports and other material concerning the duel (1835) between Turner and Stewart, lieutenants on the U.S.S. Delaware, that ended in Stewart's death. Includes letters or statements from Simon B. Bissell, George Jones, John H. Marshall, Thomas Turner, and William Turk to John B. Nicolson, commander of the U.S.S. Delaware, and Daniel T. Patterson, commander of the U.S. Naval Forces in the Mediterranean.

Deposited by the Naval Historical Foundation, 1949.

U.S.S. President Lincoln Club

Records, 1918–68. 500 items.

TSS. of statements by crew members captured after the sinking of the U.S.S. President Lincoln, annual memorial observations of the club, crew rosters, and newspaper clippings. Includes correspondence and diary (1918) of Percy Wright Foote (1879–1961), commanding officer of the ship.

Deposited by the Naval Historical Foundation, 1972.

United States.   Naval Observatory

Records, 1833–1900. 10,000 items.

Correspondence, supplemented by reports, purchase orders, bills of lading, receipts, printed matter, and miscellany, chiefly relating to the publication of the monthly American Ephemeris and Nautical Almanac; printing and distribution of wind and current charts of the Atlantic, Pacific, and Indian Oceans; functioning of the observatory's library; and participation in the International Exhibition of 1876. Subjects include astronomy, navigational aids and equipment, and building alterations. Principal staff correspondents include J. H. C. Coffin, Charles Henry Davis, George Manning, Matthew Fontaine Maury, Simon Newcomb, and Joseph Winlock. Other correspondents include Cleveland Abbe, William Beebe, William Chauvenet, Alvan Clark, James A. Garfield, David Gill, Joseph Henry, George William Hill, Elias Loomis, Maria Mitchell, Benjamin Peirce, Charles Saunders Peirce, John Daniel Runkle, Truman Henry Safford, Ainsworth Rand Spofford, Benjamin Franklin Stevens, Sears Cook Walker, James Craig Watson, and Gideon Welles.

Deposited by the Naval Historical Foundation, 1951.

United States.   Naval War College

Records, 1884–1914. 27 items.

In part, photocopies.

Chiefly letters to Stephen B. Luce and Henry C. Taylor during their terms as President of the Naval War College, discussing such matters as the curriculum, lecturers, appropriations, and a proposal for a school with post-graduate courses for naval officers. Correspondents include Charles C. Cornwell, Alfred T. Mahan, Thomas Perry, David D. Porter, Francis M. Ramsay, and William L. Rodgers.

Deposited by the Naval Historical Foundation, 1955.

United States. Navy
Collection, 1899–1933. 6 items.

Report (1899) of a tour of the Philippine Islands, headed by Jacob G. Schurman, president of the Philippine Commission; speech (ca. 1903) by an inhabitant of Tutuila, American Samoa, to officers of the U.S. Navy requesting the return of Benjamin F. Tilley to be their governor; letter (1920) of a veteran of the Confederate Army recalling capture and subsequent treatment of Confederate soldiers by U.S. naval and Army parties; list (1933) of Benedict Arnold's squadron compiled by Howard Irving Chapelle; letter (n. d.) to Thomas Shock, U.S. naval engineer; and book of orders for unknown ship (n. d.).

Deposited by the Naval Historical Foundation, 1964.

United States. Navy Dept.
Collection, 1840–63. 10 items.

Official letters from Navy commissioners and other personnel of the Navy Dept. to naval officers, and records of examinations of medical personnel. Correspondents include William Ballard Preston and Charles Stewart.

Deposited by the Naval Historical Foundation, 1964.

United States Navy submarines collection
Collection, 1936. 10 items.

Reports and newspaper clippings of disposal by sinking of the U.S. Navy submarines, the S–4 and S–19.

Deposited by the Naval Historical Foundation, 1964.

United States Navy Yard, Charlestown, Mass.
Collection, 1801–05. 14 items.

Payroll lists for carpenters, laborers, and mastmakers, including two lists for repairs made on the U.S.F. Constitution. Some of the lists are signed by Samuel Nicholson, first superintendent, U.S. Navy Yard, Charlestown, Mass.

Deposited by the Naval Historical Foundation, 1964.

Vroom, Guysbert B., b. 1778
Notebook, 1791–99. 1 v. (216 p.)

Naval officer. School exercise book kept by Vroom which contains mathematical exercises and essays; and letterbook copies of outgoing correspondence.

Deposited in the Library by Guysbert Vroom in 1924; transferred to the Naval Historical Foundation, 1951.

Wainwright family
Papers, 1842–1941. 18 items.

Naval officers. Letters, 1842–48, of Richard Wainwright (1817–1862) to his family; typescript or holograph articles on naval topics, 1924 and undated, by Richard Wainwright (1849–1926); and carbon copy of a letter to Richard Wainwright (1881–1944) from Dudley W. Knox, May 27, 1941.

Deposited by the Naval Historical Foundation, 1949.

Walker, John Grimes, 1835–1907
Papers, 1873–1903. 1750 items.

Naval officer. General and official letterbooks, chiefly 1885–94, relating to family matters and Walker's tours of duty.

Register published by the Library in 1970.

Deposited by the Naval Historical Foundation, 1964.

Watson, John Crittenden, 1842–1923
Papers, 1845–1960. 1500 items.

Naval officer. General and family correspondence, notes, reports, official orders, newspaper clippings, photos, and scrapbooks, chiefly 1884–1923, relating to Watson's service in the Civil War, his postwar duty with the European Squadron, his command of the U.S.S. Wyoming, his controversy with William E. Chandler, Secretary of the Navy, over the dismissal of civilian employees at the Brooklyn Navy Yard in 1883, his command of the Asiatic station, and his special assignment in Europe. Includes papers of Watson's sons, Edward H. Watson, naval officer, and James T. Watson, Army officer. James' papers include correspondence and notes concerning cases to be tried by the Judge Advocate, and Edward's papers relate to the Honda disaster in 1923 and the ensuing court of inquiry. Correspondents include Willard H. Brownson, Silas Casey, George Dewey, David G. Farragut, William T. Meredith, David D. Porter, and Theodore Roosevelt.

Register published by the Library in 1968.

Deposited by the Naval Historical Foundation, 1967.

Webster, Harrie, 1843-1921
Papers, 1889–1913. 50 items.

Naval officer. Correspondence, articles, autobiography, photos, notes, lyrics, and other papers, relating, in part, to the wreck of the U.S.S. Vandalia, on which Webster served as an engineer, John Paul Jones, the Spanish-

American War, the U.S.S. Illinois, and Webster's Civil War service under David Farragut in the Battle of Mobile Bay.

Deposited by the Naval Historical Foundation, 1967.

Welles, Roger,   1862–1932

Papers, 1884–1926. 2100 items.

Naval officer. Correspondence, journals, orders to duty, article and speech file, diary of Welles' wife, newspaper clippings, printed matter, and miscellany, chiefly 1891–1926, relating to Welles' duties as special representative for the World's Columbian Exposition, as director of naval intelligence, and as commander of the Asiatic and Atlantic Fleets and of the U.S. Naval Forces in Europe. Correspondents include James Nicholls Allison, Robert Woods Bliss, Victor Blue, Robert Edward Coontz, Josephus Daniels, Alexander Pollock Moore, and Albert Parker Niblack.

Finding aid in the Library.

Deposited by the Naval Historical Foundation, 1949.

Wells, Tom Henderson,   1917–

Notes. 1500 items.

Naval officer and author. Carbon copies of research notes for Wells' book *Commodore Moore and the Texas Navy* (1960); together with an index to the notes.

Finding aid in the Library.

Deposited by the Naval Historical Foundation, 1963.

Welsh, George P.,   d. 1860

Papers, ca. 1771–1851. 7 items.

Naval officer. Official journals, MS. manual on sailing and astronomy (ca. 1771), and printed matter. Journals were kept by Welsh on his midshipman cruises on the U.S.F. Brandywine, Mediterranean Squadron (1841–42), U.S.S. Independence, Home Squadron (1843), U.S.S. Levant, Pacific Squadron (1843–45); and U.S.S. Plymouth, East India Squadron (1848–51). Journal kept on the U.S.S. Levant includes maps and sketches (profile), and the U.S.S. Plymouth journal includes extensive commentary on the negotiations and visits of U.S. special agent Joseph Balestier in Cochin China, Siam, Subi, and Borneo.

Deposited by the Naval Historical Foundation, 1964.

Welsh, George Silvis

Papers, 1879–80. 2 items.

Naval officer. Navigation book, U.S.F. Constellation, November 1879, U.S.S. Trenton, December 1879, and U.S.S. Quinnebaug, September 1880;

and watch, quarter, fire, boat, battalion, station bills, etc., of the U.S.S. Trenton, January 1880.

Deposited by the Naval Historical Foundation, 1964.

Whiting, William Henry, 1843–1925

Papers, 1731–1952. 500 items.

Naval officer. Genealogical data; 18th century documents including letters, bills of sale, and a petition; steel engravings, photos, and tintypes; and newspaper clippings and printed matter. The bulk of the material covers the period 1842–1900 and consists of genealogical information concerning the Whiting family in Great Britain and the U.S. and the family's relationship to George Washington.

Finding aid in the Library.

Deposited by the Naval Historical Foundation, 1960, 1964.

Wilkinson, Theodore Stark, 1888–1946

Papers, 1942–45. 200 items.

In part, transcripts (typewritten)

Naval officer. Personal and official correspondence, diary, orders to duty, awards, citations, transcripts of radio broadcasts, memoranda, and clippings, relating to Wilkinson's duties as deputy commander, South Pacific area. Diary describes operations at Bougainville, Palau, and Leyte, and Wilkinson's tour of duty in Japan after the surrender. Conferences with William F. Halsey are recorded as well as visits by Richard E. Byrd, Raymond Clapper, Hans V. Kaltenborn, Henry C. Lodge, Carl Mydans, Ogden Reid, and Eleanor Roosevelt. Correspondents include Harold E. Barrowclough, Claude R. Branch, Frederick H. Brooke, Robert B. Carney, George H. Fort, Oscar W. Griswold, William F. Halsey, John R. Hodge, Randall Jacobs, James Kendall, Thomas C. Kinkaid, Alan G. Kirk, Chester Nimitz, Richmond K. Turner, Nathan F. Twining, Alexander A. Vandegrift, and Hugh M. Wilkinson.

Deposited by the Naval Historical Foundation, 1967, 1972.

Williams, Charles E.

Papers, 1904–16. 11 items.

Naval engineer. Correspondence, blueprints, and printed matter relating to the installation of wireless telegraph or radio equipment.

Deposited by the Naval Historical Foundation, 1968.

Williams, Henry, b. 1877

Papers, 1896–98. 20 items.

Naval officer. Letters of Henry Williams to his father, Thomas John Chew Williams, concerning the bombardment, blockade, and landing of soldiers

in Cuba; the blockade of Puerto Rico; and other matters relating to the
Spanish-American War. Also a letter (with translation) to T. J. C. Williams
from Pascual Cervera y Topete, a prisoner of war at the U.S. Naval Academy.
Deposited by the Naval Historical Foundation, 1952.

Wilson, John Clark,   d. 1923
Letter, 1898. 1 item.
Naval officer. Letter (Dec. 15, 1898) of Wilson, U.S.S. Vixen, Navy
Yard, Norfolk, Va., to Mrs. William A. Maury, concerning the sending of
a signal lantern from the Spanish cruiser Reina Mercedes.
Deposited by the Naval Historical Foundation, 1964.

Wilson, Samuel Lewis,   1844–1879
Papers, 1862–1939. 22 items.
In part, transcripts.
Naval officer. Letter from Wilson to his cousin, Lizzie Wilson, concern-
ing his life at the U.S. Naval Academy and family matters. Also letters
concerning Wilson's death and burial place in Yokohama, Japan.
Deposited by the Naval Historical Foundation, 1964.

Winslow, Francis,   1818–1862
Journal, 1834–37. 1 item.
Naval officer. Holograph journal (with photocopy) relating to his train-
ing as a midshipman on the U.S.F. Brandywine, U.S.S. Natchez, and U.S.S.
Erie, Brazil Station. Includes descriptions of the officers and the conversa-
tions aboard ship and of the cities of Rio de Janeiro, Montevideo, and
Buenos Aires.
Deposited by the Naval Historical Foundation, 1969.

Winslow, John Ancrum,   1811–1873
Collection, 1864–88. 10 items.
In part, photocopies.
Naval officer. Logbook of the U.S.S. Kearsarge, commanded by Capt.
Winslow, containing an account of the battle (June 19, 1864) in which
the C.S.S. Alabama was sunk off the coast of Cherbourg, France, together
with articles, photos, and other material relating to the battle.
Deposited by the Naval Historical Foundation, 1969.

Wise, Henry Augustus,   1819–1869
Papers, 1850–69. 90 items.
Naval officer and author. General correspondence, scrapbook of newspaper clippings, photos, sketches, and other papers, chiefly relating to Wise's
books. Correspondents include James Black, Gustavus Fox, John H. Hill,

Jonas Hill, Matthew F. Maury, and Edward Maynard.
Deposited by the Naval Historical Foundation, 1949.

Wood family
Papers, 1836–1906, of William W. Wood (1816–1882) and of his son, Thomas Newton Wood (1854–1919). 28 items.

The papers of William W. Wood, naval officer, consist of correspondence, including three letters from Franklin Harper Elmore; indenture of Wood's apprenticeship to West Point Foundry Association; and printed matter. The papers of Thomas Newton Wood, marine officer, consist of correspondence with Anderson C. Quisenberry and Edwin Longnecker; a diary he kept as a student at the U.S. Naval Academy; a notebook (1873) describing the East Indies, Morocco, and Japan; an unpublished article (1891) entitled The Marines; commissions; and a scrapbook (1872–84) containing newspaper clippings, photos, telegrams, and visiting cards.
Deposited by the Naval Historical Foundation, 1964.

Woodworth, Selim Edwin, 1815–1871
Papers, 1851–65. 4 items.
Photocopies.
Naval officer. Letter, dated Oct. 25, 1865, describing Woodworth's service in the U.S. Navy (1838–64); list of the various naval posts held by Woodworth; certificate of membership on the San Francisco Committee of Vigilance, dated June 9, 1851; and a photo of Woodworth.
Deposited by the Naval Historical Foundation, 1964.

Worden, John Lorimer, 1818–1897
Papers, 1861–98. 65 items.
In part, transcripts.
Naval officer. Letters exchanged between Samuel F. Du Pont and Gideon Welles concerning Worden's incarceration as a prisoner of war (1861) and his service in the South Atlantic Blockading Squadron (1863); letter to Worden from William Reynolds concerning the squadron's visits to German ports; general orders, mostly issued by Worden as superintendent of the U.S. Naval Academy (1869–74) and as commander of the U.S. Naval Forces, European Station (1875-77); and photo of Worden.
Deposited by the Naval Historical Foundation, 1949.

Yard, Edward M., 1809–1889
Papers, 1828–81. 2 items.
Naval officer. Official journal (222 p.) kept by Yard on the U.S.S. Fairfield, Mediterranean Station, 1828–30, with notes added in 1866 and 1881. Also a watch bill (150 p.), ca. 1838–41.
Deposited by the Naval Historical Foundation, 1950.

The following index to the 254 collections of the Naval Historical Foundation contains approximately 2,000 separate entries and represents a compilation of the names and topics in the catalog descriptions for the collections. It was produced with the assistance of electronic data processing equipment which permitted a number of economies but imposed in return a few limitations.

Each entry is succeeded by the title(s) of the collection(s) in which it appears. Name entries in the index occur in two forms: when followed by birth and death dates, the entry refers to a collection of the individual's papers; without these dates, the entry refers to a collection in which the individual is either a correspondent or a topic. "See" and "see also" entries have been supplied where appropriate.

Specific inquiries regarding material in the collections should be addressed to Library of Congress, Manuscript Division, Washington, D.C. 20540.

Index

Paullin, Charles Oscar,   1868 or 9–1944
Porter family
Riggs, Arthur Stanley,   1879–1952
Snow, Elliot,   1866–1939
Wells, Tom Henderson,   1917–
Wise, Henry Augustus,   1819–1869
Aviation
Bristol, Mark Lambert,   1868–1939
Chambers, Washington Irving,   1856–1934
Cohen, Albert Morris,   1883–1959
Fullam, William Freeland,   1855–1926
Griffin, Virgil Childers,   1891–1957
Knox, Dudley Wright,   1877–1960
Little, Charles G.,   1895–
Mustin, Henry Croskey,   1874–1923
Richardson, Holden Chester,   1878–1960
Aviation businessman
Callan, John Lansing,   1886–1958
Aviation, radio
Hooper, Stanford Caldwell,   1884–1955
Aviator
Callan, John Lansing,   1886–1958
Azore Islands, U.S. foreign relations with, 19th century
Dabney, John Bass,   d. 1826
Babbitt, Edward B.,   d. 1840
Babbitt, Edward B.,   d. 1840
Babcock, John V.
Knox, Dudley Wright,   1877–1960
Sims, William Sowden,   1858–1936
Bache, Alexander D.
Shufeldt, Robert Wilson,   1822–1895
Bache, Benjamin F.
Boarman, Charles,   1795–1879
Bache, Richard
Browning family
Badger, Charles Johnston,   1853–1932
Denig, Robert Gracy,   d. 1924
Bahamas, military bases
Greenslade, John Wills,   1880–1950
Bahn, George A.
Snow, Elliot,   1866–1939
Bainbridge, William
Bainbridge, William,   1774–1833
Bates, Richard Waller,   1892–
Gwinn, John,   1791–1849
Rodgers family
Sawyer, Horace Bucklin,   1797–1860
Shaw, John,   1773–1823
Baldridge, Harry Alexander
Baldridge, Harry Alexander,   1880–1952
Gleaves, Albert,   1858–1937
Sellers, David Foote,   1874–1949
Baldwin, Hanson W.
Knox, Dudley Wright,   1877–1960
Sellers, David Foote,   1874–1949
Baldwin, Thomas S.
Chambers, Washington Irving,   1856–1934

Balestier, Joseph
    Welsh, George P.,   d. 1860
Balfour, George
    Truxtun, Thomas,   1755–1822
Balkans, United Nations Special Committee on
    Kirk, Alan Goodrich,   1888–1963
Ballard, Henry E.
    Bates, Richard Waller,   1892–
    Boarman, Charles,   1795–1879
    Sawyer, Horace Bucklin,   1797–1860
    Selfridge, Thomas Oliver,   1804–1902
Balloons
    Chambers, Washington Irving,   1856–1934
Baltimore (U.S.S.)
    Julian, Charles
Bancroft, George
    Boarman, Charles,   1795–1879
    Gwinn, John,   1791–1849
    Pinkney, Ninian,   1811–1877
    Sawyer, Horace Bucklin,   1797–1860
    Shufeldt, Robert Wilson,   1822–1895
Barclay, Samuel M.
    Barron, James, 1769–1851
Barnes, James
    Snow, Elliot,   1866–1939
Barron, James
    Barron, James,   1769-1851
    Farragut, David Glasgow,   1801-1870
Barron, Samuel
    Dent, John Herbert,   1782–1823
Barrowclough, Harold E.
    Wilkinson, Theodore Stark,   1888–1946
Baruch, Bernard M.
    King, Ernest Joseph,   1878–1956
    McGowan, Samuel,   1870–1934
    Parsons, William Sterling,   1901–1953
Bates, John A.,   d. 1871
    Bates, John A.,   d. 1871
Bates, Jonathan
    Dickins, Francis William,   1844–1910
Bates, Richard Waller, 1892–
    Bates, Richard Waller,   1892–
Battle of Chickahominy, United States Civil War
    Gove family
Battle of Empress Augusta Bay, World War II
    Merrill, Aaron Stanton,   1890–1961
Battle of Jutland, World War I
    Gill, Charles Clifford,   1885–1948
Battle of Lake Champlain, War of 1812
    Linnet (H.M.S.)
    Stellwagen, Daniel S.,   d. 1828
Battle of Lake Erie, War of 1812
    Dorsett, Edward Lee,   1883–
    Stevens family
Battle of Manila Bay, Spanish-American War
    Carpenter, Dudley Newcomb,   b. 1874

Edison Effect, The (1961) (book)
    Bowen, Harold Gardiner,   1883–1965
Educator
    Rawson, Edward Kirk,   1846–1934
Edwards, W. Atlee
    Sims, William Sowden,   1858–1936
Eisenhower, Dwight D.
    King, Ernest Joseph,   1878–1956
Electrician, naval
    Konter, Richard Wesley,   1882–
Electronics consultant
    Hooper, Stanford Caldwell,   1884–1955
Eliot, George Fielding
    Parsons, William Sterling,   1901–1953
Eller, Ernest M.
    Furer, Julius Augustus,   1880–1963
    Merrill, Aaron Stanton,   1890–1961
Elliott, Jesse D.
    Shaw, John,   1773–1823
    Stevens family
Ellyson, Theodore G.
    Chambers, Washington Irving,   1856–1934
Elmore, Franklin H.
    Wood family
Ely, Eugene
    Chambers, Washington Irving,   1856–1934
Emmons, George D.
    McCleery, Robert W.,   d. 1863
Emory, William Hemsley
    Emory, William Hemsley,   1846–1917
    Lowe, John,   1838–1930
    Sargent, Nathan,   1849–1907
Engineer, naval
    Bowen, Harold Gardiner,   1883–1965
    United States.   Navy
    Williams, Charles E.
England, travel and description
    Chase, Philander,   1798–1824
England, U.S. assistant naval attaché
    Furer, Julius Augustus,   1880–1963
Europe, U.S. naval affairs
    Welles, Roger,   1862–1932
Evans, Robley Dunglison
    Evans, Robley Dunglison,   1846–1912
    Thomas, Charles Mitchell,   1846–1908
Evans, Walter E.
    Selfridge, Thomas Oliver,   1836–1924
Explorer
    Melville, George Wallace,   1841–1912
    Selfridge, Thomas Oliver,   1836–1924
    Shufeldt, Robert Wilson,   1822–1895
F-4 (U.S.S., submarine)
    Furer, Julius Augustus,   1880–1963
Fairfield (U.S.S.)
    Boarman, Charles,   1795–1879
    Gantt, Benjamin S.,   d. 1852
    Yard, Edward M.,   1809–1889

Roberts, Kenneth
  Sims, William Sowden, 1858–1936
Robeson, George M.
  Nicholson, Sommerville, 1822–1905
  Radford, William, 1809–1890
  Russell, John Henry, 1827–1897
Robinson, Peter B.
  McCleery, Robert W., d. 1863
Rodgers, Christopher Raymond Perry
  Nicholson, Sommerville, 1822–1905
  Stevens family
  Taylor, Henry Clay, 1845–1904
Rodgers family
  Rodgers family
Rodgers, John
  Barron, James, 1769–1851
  Bates, Richard Waller, 1892–
  Boarman, Charles, 1795–1879
  Chambers, Washington Irving, 1856–1934
  Dent, John Herbert, 1782–1823
  Dickins, Francis William, 1844–1910
  Patterson, Daniel Todd, 1786–1839
  Pook family
  Shaw, John, 1773–1823
Rodgers, John, 1773–1838
  Rodgers family
Rodgers, John, 1812–1882
  Rodgers family
Rodgers, John, 1881–1926
  Rodgers family
Rodgers, John Augustus, 1848–1933
  Rodgers family
Rodgers, Raymond P.
  Gleaves, Albert, 1858–1937
Rodgers, William L.
  Crosby, Allyn J., 1874–1955
  Meigs, John Forsyth, 1848–1924
  United States. Naval War College
Rodgers, William Ledyard, 1860–1944
  Rodgers family
Rodgers, William Tennent
  Rodgers, William Tennent
Rodman, Hugh
  Bingham, Donald Cameron, 1882–1946
Roe, Francis Asbury
  Belknap, George Eugene, 1832–1903
  Roe, Francis Asbury, 1823–1901
Roebuck (H.M.S.)
  Clark, William Bell, 1889–1968
Roosevelt, Eleanor
  Wilkinson, Theodore Stark, 1888–1946
Roosevelt, Franklin D.
  Kimmel, Husband Edward, 1882–1968
  King, Ernest Joseph, 1878–1956
  McGowan, Samuel, 1870–1934
  Nicholson, Reginald Fairfax, 1852–1939
  O'Neil, Charles, 1842–1927